HERE I STAND

HERE I STAND

PAUL ROBESON

With Lloyd L. Brown

With a New Introduction
by Sterling Stuckey

Beacon Press   Boston

Beacon Press
25 Beacon Street
Boston, Massachusetts 02108

Beacon Press books
are published under the auspices of
the Unitarian Universalist Association of Congregations.

Frontispiece photograph © Julius Lazarus

00 99 98   9 8 7

Library of Congress Cataloging-in-Publication Data
Robeson, Paul, 1898–1976.
    Here I stand.
    1. Robeson, Paul, 1898–1976.   2. Afro-Americans
—Biography.   I. Title.
[E185.97.R63A3   1988]   305.8′96073′024   [B]   87-47882
ISBN 0-8070-6438-6
ISBN 0-8070-6445-9 (pbk.)

TO ESLANDA GOODE ROBESON

Distinguished writer and anthropologist

Thanks for many things—

*For your untiring labors in the interests of the
     African peoples,*
*For your devotion to the struggle of our folk
     here in America for full freedom,*
*For your constructive analyses of the momentous
     events at the United Nations, which affect
     all manner of human societies,*
*For the deeply shared belief in and labors for
     the attainment of a lasting peace for all
     the peoples of the earth,*
*And deepest gratitude for your help and guidance
     over many years of struggle, aspiration,
     achievement, and the constant awareness of a better
     future for our children and grandchildren.*

CONTENTS

Introduction to the 1988 Edition by Sterling Stuckey   ix

Preface by Lloyd L. Brown   xxv

Author's Foreword   1

Prologue: A Home in That Rock   6

1. I Take My Stand   28

2. "Love Will Find Out the Way"   48

3. Our Right to Travel   63

4. The Time Is Now   74

5. The Power of Negro Action   90

Epilogue: Our Children, Our World   109

Appendix   112

INTRODUCTION TO THE 1988 EDITION
Sterling Stuckey

The complex mix of forces that produced Paul Robeson's character and outlook will become apparent long before the reader has completed *Here I Stand*. Indeed, the title of the book's Prologue—"A Home in That Rock"—is from one of the great Negro spirituals and contains a world of meaning in itself:

> I got a home in that rock, don't you see (2)
> Between the earth an' sky
> Thought I heard my Savior cry
> You got a home in that rock, don't you see
>
> Poor man Lazarus, poor as I, don't you see (2)
> Poor man Lazarus, poor as I
> When he died he found a home on high
> He had a home in that rock, don't you see
>
> Rich man Dives, lived so well, don't you see (2)
> Rich man Dives, lived so well
> When he died he found a home in Hell
> He had no home in that rock, don't you see
>
> God gave Noah the rainbow sign, don't you see (2)
> God gave Noah the rainbow sign
> No more water but fire next time
> Better get a home in that rock

A discussion of Robeson's early life, "A Home in That Rock" goes far toward explaining why Robeson was later able to affirm, in remarkable measure, the revolutionary ethic at the heart of the song.

Robeson's roots were established in a religion that reveals African influences through musical creativity that allows virtually no break between the sacred and the secular; indeed, the sacred music could be said to contain seeds of the blues and jazz that bloomed in the first decade of Robeson's life. The role of the Negro home in that process deserves attention, especially when that home was, as was Paul Robeson's, headed by a minister: "Here in this little hemmed-in world where home must be theatre and concert hall and social center, there was a warmth of song. Songs of love and longing, songs of trials and triumphs, deep-flowing rivers and rollicking brooks, hymnsong and ragtime ballad, gospels and blues, and the healing comfort to be found in the illimitable sorrow of the spirituals."[1] The poor people who sang those songs and entered the makeshift theater were mainly the children of southern migrants, some of whom, like Robeson's father, were former slaves. Among Robeson's friends and playmates at such gatherings was Emma Epps, who lived across from him on Green Street in Princeton. Now ninety, she recalled recently: "Though we had trouble convincing him of it, Paul always had a voice. He could always sing."

Though he spent eight years in segregated elementary schools, in high school Robeson had positive experiences with whites, except for clashes with a racist principal who hated him for his qualities as an outstanding scholar and athlete. As a result, he regarded whites, on balance, as individuals, but he realized that most whites did not welcome competition from blacks: "From an early age I had come to accept and follow a certain protective tactic of Negro life in America, and did not fully break with the pattern until many years later. . . . Always show that you are *grateful*. (Even if what you have gained has been wrested from unwilling powers, be sure to be grateful lest 'they' take it all away.) Above all, *do nothing to give them cause to fear you.* . . ."[2]

Throughout his youth, Robeson's father insisted on "personal integrity," which included the idea of "maximum human fulfillment." These values were related to an ethical system that favored what Robeson would come to see as socialist rather than capitalist values. Success "was not to be measured in terms of money and personal advancement, but rather the goal must be the richest and highest development of one's own potential."[3]

The selflessness inherent in Reverend Robeson's outlook— and the lack of greed that it promoted—was apparent in the generosity of one black to another that so impressed Robeson in his youth. Indeed, a form of socialism was acted out in that Princeton black community, and Robeson's identification with the working class was no mere abstraction. His family— Robeson himself—was an extension of that class. "I had the closest of ties with these workers," he later wrote, "since many of my father's relatives—Uncle Ben and Uncle John and Cousin Carraway and Cousin Chance and others—had come to this town and found employment at such jobs . . . domestics in the homes of the wealthy, serving as cooks, waiters and caretakers at the university, coachmen for the town and laborers at the nearby farms and brickyards."[4] Not only were many of his relatives ex-slaves, but by the time Robeson was born ex-slaves and their children constituted almost the entire black population of America, a population not yet differentiated along class lines.

Not surprisingly, Robeson's commencement address at Rutgers, which is not treated in *Here I Stand*, gave serious consideration to the liberation of the masses of blacks, and argued that his loyalty to them was sacred. At a family reunion in Philadelphia in 1918, he spoke on "Loyalty to Convictions": "That I chose this topic was not accidental, for that was the text of my father's life—loyalty to one's convictions. Unbending. Despite anything. From my youngest days I was imbued with that concept. This bedrock idea of integrity was taught by Reverend Robeson to his children not so much by preachment . . . but, rather, by the daily example of his life and work."[5]

The brutal experiences he underwent at Rutgers put his spiritual and physical resources to an extreme test. As a freshman at the age of seventeen, he went out for the football team and his teammates tried to kill him. Providing the symbolism for his ultimate relationship to America, they ganged up on him. They broke his nose, dislocated his shoulder, and cleated his hand, tearing away all the fingernails. He considered putting football behind him but remembered that his father had impressed upon him "that when out on the football field or in a classroom or anywhere else . . . I had to show that I could take whatever they handed out. . . . This was part of our struggle."

Robeson continued to develop many of the talents that later brought him such acclaim years before he completed his undergraduate work at Rutgers, even though at no point in this process were things made easy for him. His successes in the classroom at Rutgers, and later at Columbia Law School, resulted from rigorous application of his intellect to the subjects at hand despite extraordinary demands on him from extracurricular activities ranging from athletics to acting and singing, at which he performed brilliantly. One of only two black students on the Rutgers campus during his entire four years, he was valedictorian of his class, a debating champion, and a tremendous football player, twice selected for the All-American team. Undoubtedly, his father's insistence on maximum human fulfillment was a crucial factor in the flowering of Robeson's genius. Yet the chemistry of mind and body that enabled him to achieve so much in so many fields remains one of nature's mysteries.

"A Home in That Rock" is followed by developments that occurred mainly in the post–World War II period. But flashbacks in several of the chapters that follow, especially to Robeson's London years (1927–39), provide the long view essential for understanding how his thought evolved and matured over time. It is the Prologue, however, that remains the bridge across the decades separating Robeson's formative years in New Jersey and his return to America after years abroad during a period of momentous change in the world. Robeson's narrative strategy of explaining his actions in the fifties by relying on the events of his formative years is strikingly effective.

In discussing his London years and the broadening of his intellectual and cultural horizons, Robeson frankly addresses the question of socialism and its advances in the Soviet Union. He found the Soviet Union attractive largely because he thought Africans could learn much from an experiment that, in less than twenty years, had brought many formerly "backward" people of color into the scientific/industrial world of the twentieth century. His deep interest in Africa, together with his belief in scientific socialism, was, to be sure, a source of later concern to the U.S. government, and his argument that "the power of the Soviet Union . . . would become an important factor in aiding the colonial liberation movement" seems to us now to have been prophetic.

Robeson's emphasis was on the need for people of African ancestry to take the lead in their own liberation. His essays and interviews in the thirties indicate that he no longer expected more privileged blacks to play the role he once envisioned for them. Appalled by the extent to which most were dependent on their European masters for cues on how to think and behave, he located this problem in an inferiority complex born of oppression, and urged that black students, including those from the United States, be trained in less hostile environments such as Peking or Palestine; otherwise, too few would rise above being "cardboard Europeans." His one great hope, well before his London years, was that the black masses would move forward to determine their own destiny, as Asian people were clearly already doing by the thirties.

But Robeson's concerns for people of color did not prevent him from seeing that the destinies of the oppressed are interlocked, which he discovered on the cultural plane in his years abroad. Among working people, he thought cultural connections were evident, particularly through folk music, and these connections had political consequences of which he became increasingly conscious. Just as he saw the need for blacks to have allies in America, he saw possibilities for alliances of the oppressed across geographical and racial boundaries.

Robeson, of course, enjoyed remarkable successes on the concert stages of the British Isles and Europe and won new acclaim as an actor in the theater and in films, especially in *Showboat* and in *Othello*. It was in these years that his voice took on all the power of its earlier promise. And it was then that it became, above all others, associated with the trials and triumphs of the human spirit, and therefore with the great social issues of the day: the Spanish Civil War, anti-Nazism, and the liberation of Afro-Asia.

While Robeson tells us less about his personal life in the forties than he does of other periods, his discussion of the changing context of world affairs as a consequence of World War II is superb and would have many implications for race relations in the United States then and later. Robeson felt that Afro-American resistance to oppression would be more effective in the new global context, and he became the supreme emblem of that resistance as he organized not only for civil rights in the United States but also for the liberation of Africans everywhere. But opposition was powerful, and the government, with the cooperation of various power elites, began to mount a campaign to silence and destroy him.

Shortly after his return to the United States from a concert tour in the West Indies in 1948, Robeson remarked that if he never heard another kind word, the reception he had received from his people in Jamaica and Trinidad would be sufficient to last him for the rest of his life. This sentiment, and his feeling that he had drawn his first breath of fresh air in years, was indicative of the climate for race relations and politics in the United States. Perhaps he also sensed the end of an era in his own life with the intensification of developments that were becoming increasingly ominous for the nation and the world.

In the years between his return from England in 1939 and his visit to the islands, the acclaim that he received went beyond anything he had previously known in the United States. Theodore Dreiser called him an "artistic and social genius," Walter Damrosch said that Robeson was "gifted by the gods as musician and actor," and Mark van Doren, the Shakespeare pundit at Columbia University, said, "I honor him without limit." Rockwell Kent, the artist, wrote in 1944 that he was among "countless thousands who honor [Robeson] in their hearts as few men who have ever lived have been honored."[6] By 1944, Robeson had reached the heights of his acting career with the new and lasting resonance he had given the role of Othello. In some ways, his characterization of the Moor was drawn as much from his own commanding authority in a white world as from the play itself. Informed by his consummate acting skills, Robeson's Othello was more authentic than that of any other actor of his time.

But a few years later, he set aside his career to march "up and down the nation" to protest the oppression of blacks. His fame and wealth had not softened his defense of the oppressed. Indeed, he found his people had come through their trials "unbroken . . . a race of such magnificence of spirit that there exists no power on earth that could crush them."[7] No one of the forties was more closely identified with uncompromising struggle and none had as much to lose as he. His example was unique among artists of his stature and was cause for growing concern among leaders of the white establishment at least as early as 1947.

After more than ten years abroad, he had returned with an uncanny ability to enter into and possess the songs of many peoples, his lyricism seeming to flow from some inner realm common to humanity. When his soul was at rest and set to music, his voice had about it a quiet radiance—like gold in sunlight. Such was its peculiar magic that, like daybreak, it could reach across vast distances well before revealing its full power. One doubts that power has ever been expressed more convincingly in song.

As artist and man his reputation preceded him. On the day of his arrival in Jamaica in 1948, the poet Louise Bennett wrote:

Him come at las, him deh yah chile!
Him eena newspapa!
"Paul Robeson arrives today!"
Come look pon him picksha!

Lawd wat a sight fe cure sore y'eye!
Lawd wat a tale fe tell!
Me slap eena Trelawny bush,
But me dah-feel de spell!

Him gwine ta pon Ward Theatre stage
Real-real live, wat a ting!
Him gwine fe bow, him gwine fe smile,
And den him gwine fe sing!

Him gwine fe sing! Miss Matty,
Me won' deh-deh, but me know;
Is like a garden full o' song
Eena him heart a-grow!

An doah de voice look like it dah-
Come out o' him mout part,
It soun to we like him dah-coax
De song out o' him heart.

An wen him done, de clappin an
De cheerin' from de crowd!
An every nayga head swell, every
Nayga heart feel proud!

Proud o' de man, de singer, an
Lawd, a tenkful to yuh,

Dat wen we feel proud o' him race
Dat race is fe we to![8]

But in the United States, Robeson's continued friendship
with the Soviet Union and his unyielding defense of the rights
of his people were increasingly seized upon and used in an
effort to curb his influence. In 1949, hatred of him exploded
in one of the ugliest riots of the century in Peekskill, New
York, not long after he had declared, on behalf of the youth
of Afro-Asia, that colored people did not want war with the
Soviet Union. "It is unthinkable," he said, "that American
Negroes could go to war on behalf of those who have oppressed
them for generations against the Soviet Union which in one
generation has raised our people to full human dignity" (*New
York Times*, 21 April 1949). His speech, made at the Paris
Peace Conference, was a turning point in Robeson's life; its
reception in the United States constituted a watershed in the
history of the practice of liberty and free speech in this
country.

The Establishment reaction to Robeson was largely nonracial
in one important respect: his admiration for the Soviet Union
made him, almost by reflex action, an object of hatred. But
his fame, along with his African ancestry, gave a particularly
ugly edge to that hatred. His continuing commitment to the
independence movements of colonial Africa and the uses to
which scientific socialism might be put in that process, against
the backdrop of the Paris speech, caused increasing concern
in high places. The attack on Robeson became brutal in 1949
and remained so for nearly ten years. As Lloyd Brown, Robeson's close friend and a collaborator in the writing of *Here I
Stand*, states in his preface: "And then suddenly, the spotlight
was switched off. . . . The blackout was the result of a boycott
of Robeson by the Establishment that was meant both to
silence him and to deny him any opportunity of making a

living. All doors to stage, screen, concert hall, radio, TV, and recording studio were locked against him."[9]

Robeson's salary plummeted from over $100,000 a year to less than $6,000 a year and remained there for nearly a decade. His passport was revoked, and his access to his international audience was cut off. As efforts to oppose him intensified, he fearlessly met the challenge and, under increasingly difficult conditions, worked with renewed zeal for the liberation of his people. More frequently than ever, he moved through the black communities in this country and, characteristically, took up the cause of oppressed blacks in the South, especially in Mississippi, and in Africa, especially in South Africa. He carried his message into the homes of blacks in the ghetto, discussing the issues of the day and eating at their tables. It was the kind of communion he had known from the start.

His essential orientation, brilliantly elaborated in his written work of the fifties and earlier, set him at variance with leaders of the NAACP and the Urban League. Apart from W. E. B. Du Bois, whose interests were close to his, he had little in common with national black leaders other than the desire that color prejudice be ended. It is difficult, in fact, to imagine more fundamental differences between Du Bois and Robeson and more conservative black leaders. In time, as the pressures on Robeson mounted, the failure of the black bourgeoisie to support him fueled the campaign against him. That support would have guaranteed him at least a measure of neutrality from organizations representing black people. But the forces opposing Robeson struck fear into the hearts of most black intellectuals and professionals, many of whom whispered his name for years.

Much earlier in the century, Robeson had shared with Du Bois the assumption that educated blacks, as a natural obligation, would attempt to help their people. And like Du Bois, he had not foreseen the emergence of a black middle class that would at times place its interests above the interests of black people as a whole. These miscalculations, fateful for both men, were related to Du Bois's being forced out of the NAACP in 1948 and Robeson's having to struggle to be heard by the national black community.

For the first time in history, leaders of the major rights organizations felt safe in expressing no ostensible interest in Africa. The relationship of the flowering of freedom in the United States to the rights of black people everywhere was not a concern of theirs. For them, freedom meant equal rights for blacks in the United States, nothing more. Not surprisingly, consciousness of Africa, and its influence in determining values proper to people of African ancestry in America, was threatened as never before. A new ideological and spiritual low was reached.

It was in such an atmosphere that Robeson sought to communicate his message. As he moved from one community to another, his audiences tended to be made up mainly of trade union and other working-class blacks. Many who stood before him were the spiritual descendants of the blacks of his childhood in Princeton. Before such audiences he repeatedly took up the question of African liberation, as he did in "How I Discovered Africa," in which he wrote:

> A thousand years? No, Africa's time is now! We must see that and realize what it means to us, we American brothers and sisters of the Africans. We must see that we have a part to play in helping to pry loose the robber's hold on Africa. For if we take a close look at the hands that are at Africa's throat, we will understand it all: *we know those hands.*[10]

The destiny of the colonial people of Kenya captured the interest of some members of the black rank and file and some black high school and college students. No one raised the issue with greater authority than Robeson, who had known Jomo Kenyatta personally and had a special interest in East African cultures and languages. There was no more important subject for him than African liberation, and no more important audience to which to address it. Indeed, during his London years of studying African cultures and associating with Africans, Robeson came to consider himself African. When he spoke to such audiences, few present could have known the full range of his education,[11] how deeply he had probed his spiritual heritage, and to what extent, despite his father's background of slavery, his own family was working-class. When he stood before them, it was a rare moment, a genuine hero of the working class addressing that class.

Robeson's expressions of happiness on greeting his people were at times expressions of love in a voice too gorgeous in color for the subject at hand, and the spoken word as tone poem would soon end as he began a fighting speech. On such occasions—and they were many in the fifties—the strain on his voice weighed on the minds of some who heard him, as it must have weighed on his own as the years went by, as his speeches remained lengthy and passionate. By the mid-fifties, when he was a few years away from the age of sixty, there was little indication that the repression was coming to an end, and no assurance that when it did he would still have one of the great voices of our epoch.

Even as he addressed crowds obviously devoted to him, there was a definite sense, considering the forces arrayed against him, that Robeson was isolated. As the fifties unfolded and those forces were unrelenting, his audiences were at times quite sparse. At such times he must have wondered, as he does in *Here I Stand* when discussing a black family that is threatened by a mob, "Where are the other Negroes?" Where were the Negroes when Robeson was under siege? It is a central question in the history of the Afro-American in the last half of the century.

In 1952, Robeson and Lloyd Brown began planning the work that eventually became *Here I Stand*, in which Robeson was to respond to questions about why his views were causing such concern in America. By the summer of 1957 the book had been written, and it was published the following year.

Before beginning the actual writing, Brown had spent a great deal of time observing Robeson at meetings and listening to him talk "about all the things that were of interest to him" so that his thought and language might be faithfully represented on paper.[12] After the project was finished, Robeson was satisfied that Brown had succeeded in putting him into words, as was Eslanda, Robeson's wife.

Directed primarily to ordinary blacks, the prose of *Here I Stand* is clear and at times eloquent. It is not the language of Robeson's earlier essays, which make use of a marvelous economy of expression in the service of his erudition. In fact, in essays such as "Primitives," "I Want to Be African," and "Reflections on Othello and the Nature of Our Times," the pure flame of learning lights up the page. *Here I Stand* is ideal for the audience to which it is primarily addressed, an audience that includes the black religious community, which even then was reasserting its authority in American life. And it is indispensable reading for anyone who would understand Robeson.

In establishing the context for a discussion of his politics, Robeson makes a telling remark: "At the outset, let me point out that the controversy concerning my views and actions had its origin not among the Negro people but among the white folks on top who have directed at me the thunderbolts of their displeasure and rage."[13] In a fascinating discussion of his views, he writes that through several decades—before and during the Cold War—his basic perspective on world affairs had remained the same:

More than twenty years have passed since I first visited the Soviet Union and voiced my friendly sentiments about the peoples of that land, and before that I had expressed a keen interest in the life and culture of the African peoples and a deep concern for their liberation. Indeed, before the "cold war" brought about a different atmosphere, those broader interests of mine were considered by many Negroes to be quite admirable.[14]

xxii   HERE I STAND

Even the NAACP thought his interests admirable as late as 1944 when he received its Spingarn Medal for his work on behalf of "freedom for all men." But when the larger society, following the war, changed its attitude, the NAACP changed its attitude as well. But Robeson "saw no reason" why he "should change with the weather." He tells us that he "was not raised that way."

It has now been thirty years since the publication of *Here I Stand*. The appearance of this edition comes in the year of what would have been Robeson's ninetieth birthday, twelve years after his death in 1976. The militant surge of the sixties has contributed to the creation of a very different audience for *Here I Stand* from that of the time of its first appearance. Robeson had predicted in the book that blacks, by relying mainly on their own resources, could challenge the foundations of racism in America (a theme that courses through his writings for well over two decades prior to the sixties). Another factor in the changing audience is the less hostile atmosphere in which Soviet-American relations are now being conducted.

As one looks back on the Cold War period, it is evident that America's greatest loss was the denial of freedom to very large numbers of its citizens as fear became the prevailing state of consciousness. There is no way to calculate the losses to art resulting from Robeson's virtual confinement in America. What is certain is that, in modern history, no one of comparable artistic ability has been denied freedom for so long. That denial is today a major form of persecution to be considered in discussing violations of human rights in the United States. In the final analysis, one must consider Robeson's genius as an actor as well as a singer in determining the scope of the crime that was committed against humanity, against world art.

Robeson's conception of the guiding values of a new day is resonant with meaning and demonstrates, almost painfully, the extent to which he was in advance of his times. In "Reflections on Othello and the Nature of Our Times," he states that scientists, artists, members of the professions, and liberal intellectuals "must have faith in the whole people, the emergence into full bloom of the last estate, the vision of no high and no low, no superior and no inferior—but equals, assigned to different tasks in the building of a new and richer human society."[15]

On his seventy-fifth birthday, he sent warmest thanks to friends in the United States and throughout the world, and added:

> I want you to know that I am the same Paul, dedicated as ever to the worldwide cause of humanity for freedom, peace and brotherhood. . . . Though ill health has compelled my retirement, you can be sure that in my heart I go on singing:

> "But I keeps laughing
> Instead of crying,
> I must keep fighting
> Until I'm dying,
> And Ol' Man River,
> He just keeps rolling along!"[16]

NOTES

1. *Here I Stand*, 15.
2. Ibid., 20.
3. Ibid., 18.
4. Ibid., 20.
5. Ibid., 8–9.
6. From signed documents in the Paul Robeson Archives that are quoted by Lloyd Brown in "Paul Robeson Rediscovered," *AIMS*, Occasional Paper no. 19, 1976, 6–7.
7. Paul Robeson, *Selected Writings* (Paul Robeson Archives, 1976), 65.
8. Louise Bennett, "Him Deh Yah," in *Jamaica Labrish* (Jamaica, 1966), 38. Dawn Lindo has translated the poem as follows:

> He has come at last, he is here, child!
> He is in the newspaper!
> "Paul Robeson arrives today!"
> Come and look at his picture!

Lord, what a sight to cure sore eyes!
Lord, what a tale to tell!
I am all the way in the heart of Trelawny,
But still I feel the spell!

He is going to stand on Ward Theatre stage.
In living flesh, what a thing!
He will bow, he will smile,
And then he is going to sing!

He is going to sing! Miss Matty,
I alone was there, but I know,
His voice is like a garden full of song
Growing in his heart!

And even though the voice
Seems to come out of his mouth,
It sounds to us as though he is coaxing
The song out of his heart.

And when he had finished, the clapping and
The cheering from the crowd!
And every black man's head swelled, every
Black man's heart felt proud!

Proud of the man, the singer, and
Lord, I am thankful to you,
That when we feel proud of his race,
That race is our own too!

9. *Here I Stand*, ix.
10. *Selected Writings*, 68.
11. In the fifties, Robeson took up two new and difficult languages, Arabic and Hebrew, and continued to work on others he began studying in the 1920s at the London School of Oriental Languages, where he had earned a reputation among his teachers for having a "special facility" for learning languages.
12. Interview with Lloyd L. Brown, fall 1987.
13. *Here I Stand*, 68.
14. Ibid., 29.
15. Paul Robeson, "Reflections on Othello and the Nature of Our Times," *The American Scholar* 14 (Autumn 1945):391.
16. *Selected Writings*, 96-97.

PREFACE
Lloyd L. Brown, 1971

Here I Stand, first published in 1958, was a statement of bold defiance and prophetic power. Here stood a beleaguered man who would not bend or bow; and here his muzzled voice proclaimed: *The time is now*.

For thirty years—from the First World War until after World War II—Paul Robeson's extraordinary achievements had kept him in the spotlight. First he won national fame as a football superstar—the fabulous "Robeson of Rutgers," an all-time All-American. Then he gained international renown as a concert singer and actor in starring roles on stage and screen. And then, suddenly, the spotlight was switched off. In place of the glow of stardom, a thick smokescreen was spread around him, and the giant figure of the most famous Afro-American of that era could no more be seen.

The blackout was the result of a boycott of Robeson by the Establishment that was meant both to silence him and to deny him any opportunity of making a living. All doors to stage, screen, concert hall, radio, TV, and recording studio were locked against him. By denying him a passport and decreeing that he could not leave the country even for travel not requiring a passport (such as to Canada, the West Indies and Mexico), the Federal government barred Robeson from continuing his career abroad.

Though he was banished as a performing artist and denied his rights as a citizen, Robeson was never charged with any illegal action; he was never arrested or put on trial. But his persecutors made no bones about why he was being punished: Robeson, they said, was a dangerous Red. Robeson, they said, was a dangerous Black. That made him twice as bad as anyone else in the "Fearful Fifties," when Communism at home and abroad was said to be a clear and present danger to the American Way of Life.

Speaking to a Harlem audience in that period, the eminent Afro-American historian W. E. B. Du Bois, himself a victim of the anti-Communist witchhunt, contrasted Robeson's continuing worldwide popularity with his banishment at home. Dr. Du Bois said of Robeson: "He is without doubt today, as a person, the best known American on earth, to the largest number of human beings. His voice is known in Europe, Asia and Africa, in the West Indies and South America and in the islands of the seas. Children on the streets of Peking and Moscow, Calcutta and Jakarta greet him and send him their love. Only in his native land is he without honor and rights."

Here I Stand, which now reappears after being out of print for a decade, is indispensable for an understanding of Paul Robeson's viewpoint. It was written, he said, "to set the record straight," and to answer the questions: "Who, What and Why is Paul Robeson?"

When his book was published, however, the "Big White Folks," whom Robeson had defied, made a concerted effort to boycott the book and thus silence his voice in print as they had silenced him in all the other mass media. In one area that boycott achieved a near-total success: with one insignificant exception, *no white commercial newspaper or magazine in the entire country so much as mentioned Robeson's book.* Leading papers in the field of literary coverage, like *The New York Times* and the *Herald-Tribune,* not only did not review it; they refused even to include its name in their lists of "books out today."

Recently, when this writer asked the *Times* about the matter, the present Sunday Editor, Daniel Schwarz, wrote in reply: "We have tried to find some record of what happened to Paul Robeson's book, 'Here I Stand,' but our files do not go that far back. . . . I am told that Paul Robeson's book doesn't appear in the listings of the Book Review Digest, so apparently it was not only The Times Book Review which decided not to review the book. I just want to assure you that we carefully consider every book we receive and I am certain that any book by Paul Robeson would not have been rejected for review if in the judgment of the editors it merited attention."

Even if one could imagine, however, that every editor of the American white press, individually and without pressure, came to the same judgment that Robeson's book did not merit attention, there exists an overwhelming fact to prove that their unanimity was not a miraculous coincidence. That fact is this: *In two other areas, which were beyond the control of the boycotters, many editors came to an altogether different judgment.*

One of these areas was the world beyond the U.S. borders that Robeson was forbidden to cross. Although *Here I Stand* was addressed primarily to black Americans, reviewers in all the many lands where the book was republished found that it *did* merit attention. Nor was this judgment limited to the Soviet Union and other socialist countries where Robeson had long been a legendary hero. Unlike the liberal *Times* in New York, the Tory *Times* in London reviewed the book (August 14, 1958). Noting that "Robeson is a single-minded crusader, his mission is to secure equal social and political rights for the American Negro," the London reviewer went on to say that his book "commands attention because he is a great artist, because he is accused of Communism, and because, by refusing him a passport for many years, the American government promoted him to the status of a political martyr."

Another striking example of that different judgment was the widespread attention that the Japanese edition of *Here I Stand* received. In a note accompanying a batch of laudatory reviews printed in Japan's leading papers, the translator, Akira

Iwasaki, reported to Robeson's U.S. publisher: "The book got a very good critical appraisal. It was more than I expected, since the 'bourgeois' newspapers and magazines here usually omit to mention the works of progressive artists. But they were impressed by the personal integrity of Mr. Robeson."

In India, the mass-circulation tabloid, *Blitz*, published (April 5, 1958) a four-page illustrated supplement which, under the headline "Black Voice of God," was devoted entirely to Robeson's book. The editor felt that the book not only merited attention but called for action as well. "We must take Robeson's slogan, THE TIME IS NOW," he wrote, "and arrange mass demonstrations to show that we completely and solidly support the cause of the American Negro."

Far more significant than the response abroad, however, was the response in the second large area where the anti-Robeson ban was broken—in the black communities of America. The breakthrough began in Harlem where Othello Associates, an independent Negro publishing company, brought out Robeson's book. (It might be noted that among the many meaningful misstatements in Edwin P. Hoyt's recent biography of Robeson was that author's assertion that *Here I Stand* was published abroad by a white publisher. The fact is, the British edition Hoyt cites, and all the other foreign editions, were produced by arrangement with the black U.S. publisher.)

What followed the publication of Robeson's book was a development altogether unprecedented in the period of McCarthyite repression: an important section of the Afro-American press moved with speed and energy to publicize and promote the sale of a book that expressed the ideas of a man considered by the dominant class to be Enemy Number One. The fact that the Negro editors were well aware of the source of the anti-Robeson ban was indicated by a Chicago *Crusader* editorial (March 8, 1958) that referred scornfully to certain "other Negro editors [who,] scared that Washington might send the F.B.I. to check on them, took to their heels whenever 'he name of Robeson was mentioned."

The Baltimore *Afro-American* (with editions in several other cities), took the lead in the widespread defiance of the ban. As soon as *Here I Stand* was off the press, the *Afro* began its forceful campaign to get a hearing for it. That effort started with an editorial (February 22, 1958) that hailed Robeson's "remarkable book," and announced that the *Afro's* magazine section would serialize several of its chapters. Then came the five-part series, starting with the March 15 issue, which also featured a notable review of *Here I Stand* by Saunders Redding. (Later, in his annual year-end roundup for the paper, on January 10, 1959, Redding listed Robeson's book among the ten works that "impressed this reviewer most strongly in 1958.")

The *Afro* followed up (May 3) with a second editorial, titled "The Paul Robeson Story," that deservedly took "some pardonable pride" in the fact that the first printing of *Here I Stand* was sold out in the first six weeks. The editorial noted that Robeson had chosen a "different technique from that of more orthodox leaders," and justified the paper's support of him by asserting: "In fighting slavery, John Brown and Frederick Douglass resorted to different methods, but they were both on the same side."

The late Carl Murphy, who as the *Afro-American's* president directed this campaign, was joined by the parallel efforts made by another leading black journalist, P. L. Prattis, then chief editor of the Pittsburgh *Courier*. The fact that the influential *Courier* was a close second to the *Afro* in defying the ban against Robeson was largely due to the integrity of Prattis, who, along with Murphy, had earlier dared to condemn the frame-up of Dr. Du Bois when few others would do so.

The main front-page headline in the *Courier* of February 22, 1958, was: "PAUL ROBESON STATES HIS CASE," and the cover story of its magazine section of that date dramatized the news that Robeson had written an important book. Though the *Courier* published no review of the book (probably a friendly act, since the book editor was the arch-conservative George S.

Schuyler), Prattis devoted his column (March 29, 1958) to a
discussion of *Here I Stand.* His paper printed numerous news
stories about the successful campaign to sell the book, as well
as many enthusiastic letters from Robeson's readers.

The only negative review of *Here I Stand* that this writer
knows about appeared in the March, 1958, issue of the
N.A.A.C.P.'s magazine, *The Crisis,* and was written by its
editor. The book was deemed to be "disorderly and confusing"
and its author was described as a man whom "Negroes . . .
never regarded as a leader," and who "imagines his misfortunes
to stem, not from his own bungling, but from the persecution
of 'the white folks on top.'" (However, the founding editor of
The Crisis, Dr. Du Bois, evidently shared Robeson's alleged
delusion, since he said at the time: "The persecution of Paul
Robeson by the government . . . has been one of the most
contemptible happenings in modern history." [*Autobiography
of W. E. B. Du Bois,* p. 396].)

An opposite view to that of *The Crisis* on Robeson's persecution and his status as a leader was given by the Chicago
Crusader, which devoted most of its editorial page (March 8,
1958) to a lengthy statement titled "Paul Robeson: A Man."
Welcoming his book, the editorial said: "We have thought all
along that the great singer, athlete and lawyer, as well as
freedom fighter, has been persecuted because he wouldn't bow
down to the white folks." On the subject of his leadership, the
Crusader asserted: "Paul Robeson has been one of the mightiest
of all Negro voices raised against world oppression of people
based on race, color, nationality and religion. He is known
wherever there are people as a champion of the rights of man."

The editorial had more to say on that subject:

> There are times in our struggle for full equality when stal-
> wart men like Robeson, carved in the heroic mould of
> Cudjo, Fred Douglass, Jack Johnson, Dr. Ossian Sweet of
> Detroit, and Oscar DePriest of Chicago, are needed for
> the physical example. This is the kind of leadership that
> Paul Robeson lives and sings about that will get Negroes

off their knees where they are being executed daily before the firing squad of racial prejudice, discrimination, Jim Crow and anti-Negro terrorism, onto their own two legs on which they must stand like men and fight this thing out toe to toe. White folks are scared of this type of leadership. They feared it in Edward H. Wright in Chicago, Wright Cuney in Texas and Ben Davis in Georgia. They were enraged at Jack Johnson who could look a white man in the eye in such a way as to make him cringe. In Paul Robeson they have met their match again.

Not all reviewers could be that outspoken, and in some cases they quoted at length Robeson's most militant statements without making any comment. In one case, the reviewer (Buddy Lonesome in the St. Louis *Argus,* April 25, 1958) quoted various paragraphs from Chapter 4 ("The Time Is Now"), and Chapter 5 ("The Power of Negro Action"), which he saw as "particularly pertinent." Then he came to a key point in the latter chapter where he felt that Robeson had gone too far. However, in stating his disagreement, the reviewer strongly hinted that he had in fact got the message:

"He [the author] gives an example of a Negro family huddling in their newly purchased home while a mob of howling bigots mills around the house. Robeson then candidly asks, 'Where are the other Negroes?' There I differ with him, for it certainly wouldn't be right or meet for Negroes to rush to arms, thereby creating another mob, to still the howls of the indignant white bigots. But then I remember the indulgent smirks of Americans around the country when Indians in Lumbee, N.C., grabbed rifles to rout a klavern of white-sheeted ku kluxers, and I pause for deep reflection."

The most analytical assessment of Robeson's ideas on the black liberation struggle that appeared in the Negro press was the review in the Los Angeles *Herald-Dispatch* (May 8, 1958). The reviewer, William C. Taylor, focused attention on Chapter 5, which, he said, "by itself makes this book a 'must' on every reading list." He noted that, "while strongly advocating unity of Negro and white, Robeson warns of a 'rising resentment against the control of our affairs by white people, regardless of whether that domination is expressed by the blunt orders of political bosses or more discreetly by the 'advice' of white liberals which must be heeded or else.' "

Along with his insistence that the liberation movement must be led by an independent black leadership, Robeson had stressed that another quality was also needed: "To live in freedom one must be prepared to die to achieve it. . . . He who is not prepared to face the trials of battle will never lead to a triumph." To the Los Angeles reviewer Robeson's ideas on this subject were "right down the alley," and he quoted the following passage as being especially meaningful: "The primary quality that Negro leadership must possess, as I see it, is *a single-minded dedication to their people's welfare* . . . for the true leader all else must be subordinated to the interests of those whom he is leading." (Emphasis in original.)

In addition to much of the black press, the left-wing newspapers and magazines of the country also considered that Robeson's book merited attention. Among the reviewing publications in this area and their respective writers were: *National Guardian,* Cedric Belfrage (March 10, 1958); *New World Review,* Louis E. Burnham (May, 1958); *Mainstream,* Shirley Graham (March, 1958); and *The Worker,* Phillip Bonosky (May 4, 1958). The principal Marxist response to *Here I Stand* appeared in *Political Affairs* (April, 1958, pp. 1–8). The reviewer was the late Benjamin J. Davis, a noted black militant, Communist Party leader, and son of the Ben Davis of Georgia whose leadership was praised in the above-quoted review in the Chicago *Crusader.*

Davis asserted that with the publication of *Here I Stand* "a new dimension is added to the massive array of Robeson's contributions to the goal of human dignity," and he described the book as "beautifully, simply and movingly written, bold in conception, sound in content, broad in approach." Noting that there was a "conspiracy of muteness on the part of the monopoly press" regarding the book, Davis said that the reason for the boycott was that Robeson's book "brings forward a people's program of action which, if seized upon by the Negro people and their allies, could not fail to have the most profound positive effects upon the present struggles of the Negro for dignity and full citizenship."

The Marxist reviewer discussed one aspect of the author's stand that had been skipped over by the non-Left reviewers, namely, that "Robeson makes no bones about his friendship with the Soviet Union" and the other socialist countries. He quoted the passage where Robeson wrote of "my deep conviction that for all mankind a socialist society represents an advance to a higher stage of life—that it is a form of society which is economically, socially, culturally, and ethically superior to a system based upon production for private profit."

Perhaps the core of Davis's assessment was this: "Communists, in particular," he wrote, "should learn from the opinions of others, especially those outside their ranks, who, like Robeson, are participants in, fighters for, and students of the struggle for a better life. . . . A strong partisan of socialism, he, nevertheless, recognizes that the attainment of the Negro's full citizenship is a massive struggle requiring the unity of people of diverse views and parties on a common program of action. . . . Robeson's book introduces into the market place of ideas the basic question of how one who believes in the principles of scientific socialism can project a program broader and more effective than any yet advanced on the American scene by any people's leader."

In concluding this survey of the response to *Here I Stand,* a few words from the present writer may be in order. I am grateful that I had the opportunity to serve as Robeson's collaborator in the writing of his book and to be one of the "Othello Associates" who published it. It has been gratifying to see that many of Robeson's militant ideas have been taken up by today's liberation movement and that many young people are finding their way along paths blazed by this great man of whom most of them have never heard.

Unfortunately, however, when young people do hear of him they usually hear only the testimony of his enemies. For example, students are often directed to Harold Cruse's *The Crisis of the Negro Intellectual,* a book that strikes me as giving a thoroughly false picture of Robeson, one that would make young black militants scorn a man they would honor if they knew the truth. For instance, on page 297 Cruse writes: "As I have pointed out, the Negro-actor-performer-singer has always developed an ambivalent communion (or none at all) with the Negro creative artist—upon whom the interpreters seldom depend for their artistic accomplishments or financial status." Incredibly, the prime example Cruse gives to illustrate his dubious generalization is—Paul Robeson!

On the other hand, students have not been directed to the primary source, Robeson himself, where they could learn the truth. Cruse's above-cited statement is contradicted by Robeson's own account (see Chapter 2 herein) of how his artistic career was based upon the black cultural heritage. After describing the decisive influence on his career that was made by the noted black composer and arranger Lawrence Brown, Robeson points out that "for my first five years as a singer my repertoire consisted entirely of my people's songs."

With characteristic modesty, Robeson does not mention that he was in fact *the first concert singer to present a program comprised only of songs composed and arranged by Afro-Americans.* The date of his first concert, April 19, 1925, deserves to be commemorated as one of the most important events in American musical history. (With rare insight and vision, the music critic of the New York *World* wrote on that occasion: "All those who listened last night to the first concert in this country made entirely of Negro music . . . may have been present at a turning point, one of those thin points of time in which a star is born and not yet visible—the first appearance of this folk wealth to be made without deference or apology.")

Any honest appraisal would show that Robeson's internationalism, his all-embracing humanism, was developed *through* his deep communion with the Afro-American heritage. Indeed, twenty years ago the present writer, arguing that the Negro creative writer could best reach the goal of universality by basing his work on the cultural heritage of his own people, cited Robeson as a living example of that achievement. I wrote:

"A giant figure in our country exemplifies this concept in another field of the arts—Paul Robeson. Here is a man who is the foremost people's artist of America and a world artist. He sings the songs of the peoples of the world in the languages of those peoples and touches their hearts; they call him brother, son. And what is the primary source of his universal art? His people. His art is great for it has a great foundation—the rich national culture and psychology of the Negro people: sorrow song and jubilee, work song and dance song." (*Masses & Mainstream,* April, 1951, p. 54.)

The record also shows that not only as an artist but as an activist Robeson firmly based himself on Afro-American tradition. Thus when he was summoned before the House Un-American Activities Committee, one of the Congressional inquisitors asked why, if he liked Russia so much, he had not stayed there. Robeson's retort came quick as a fighter's counterpunch: "Because my father was a slave, and my people died to build this country, and I'm going to stay right here and have a part of it, just like you. And no fascist-minded people like you will drive me from it. Is that clear?"

Those defiant words of 1956 recall a similar statement made in 1829 by David Walker, author of the first Afro-American book to call for the overthrow of the system of slavery. In Walker's *Appeal to the Colored Citizens of the World,* the author, urging his fellows to resist all colonization schemes, declared: "Let no man of us budge one step . . . America is more our country than it is the whites' . . . The greatest riches in all America have arisen from our blood and tears — and will they drive us from our property and homes, which we have earned with our *blood?*"

David Walker, we are told, died mysteriously; and it was suspected that those whom he denounced as the "slave-holding party, our oppressors and murderers" had somehow brought about his death. In Robeson's case there can be no doubt that the "fascist-minded people" whom he challenged did all they could to obscure the man and his message.

It can be expected, however, that the inquiring minds of the new generation will break through to the truth about him. Inevitably, like a mountain peak that becomes visible as the mist is blown away, the towering figures of Paul Robeson will emerge as the thick white fog of lies and slanders is dispelled. Then he will be recognized and honored here in his homeland, as he is throughout the world, as Robeson the Great Forerunner.

New York
April 9, 1971

AUTHOR'S FOREWORD

I AM A NEGRO. The house I live in is in Harlem—this city within a city, Negro metropolis of America. And now as I write of things that are urgent in my mind and heart, I feel the press of all that is around me here where I live, at home among my people.

Not far away is the house where my brother Ben lives: the parsonage of Mother A.M.E. Zion Church of which Ben —Reverend Benjamin C. Robeson—has been pastor for many years. My brother's love which enfolds me is a precious, living bond with the man, now forty years dead, who more than anyone else influenced my life—my father, Reverend William Drew Robeson. It is not just that Ben is my older brother, but he reminds me so much of Pop that his house seems to glow with the pervading spirit of that other Reverend Robeson, my wonderful, beloved father.

Next door to the parsonage is the church where on Sunday mornings I am united with the fellowship of thousands of my people, singing with them their songs, feeling the warmth of their handshakes and smiles—this too is a link with my earliest days, the congregations I grew up in as a boy in Princeton, in Westfield, in Somerville.

And more: here is a bond that joins me with the long, hard march that is my people's history in America. This very church, Mother Zion, the mother church of the great African Methodist Episcopal Zion denomination, goes all the way back to 1796 when it was founded by free Negroes who could not abide the church of the Christian slave-masters. Sojourner Truth, heroine of our liberation struggle, was an early member of Mother Zion; and Frederick Douglass, our greatest hero and teacher, and Harriet Tubman, our Moses of the Underground Railroad, also played their part in the glorious tradition of our church.

Yes, I've got a home in that rock!

The streets outside are alive with the presence of my people . . . the rhythms of their footsteps, their laughter, their greetings to one another. I, who have heard only a few miles away, at Peekskill, the baying of the lynch-mob, the cries for my life from hate-twisted mouths, feel here the embrace of love. *Hello, Paul—it's good to see you! It's good to have you back!*

And it's so good to be back. For this is my community. Every street and landmark around here is rich with memories of the good times and dreams of young manhood . . . Harlem after the first world war. Here I met and married Essie; here lifelong friendships began; here I started my career as an artist. Just a few blocks away, at the YWCA, I first walked on the stage in a play; and here I sang, for fun, in the clubs and cabarets; here were the thrills of the big basketball games, the dances, the social life. . . . Yes, here is my homeground—here and in all the Negro communities throughout the land. Here I stand.

I am an American. From my window I gaze out upon a scene that reminds me how deep-going are the roots of my people in this land. Across the street, carefully preserved as an historic shrine, is a colonial mansion that served as a headquarters for General George Washington in 1776, during the desperate and losing battles to hold New York against the advancing British. The winter of the following year found Washington and the ragged remnants of his troops encamped at Valley Forge, and among those who came to offer help in that desperate hour was my great-great-grandfather. He was Cyrus Bustill, who was born a slave in New Jersey and had managed to purchase his freedom. He became a baker and it is recorded that George Washington thanked him for supplying bread to the starving Revolutionary Army.

Yes, for well over 300 years my people have been a part of American life and history. A half-century has passed since W. E. B. Du Bois, in his classic *The Souls of Black Folk*, challenged white Americans in these words of poetry and truth:

> "Your country? How came it yours? Before the Pilgrims landed we were here. Here we have brought our three gifts and mingled them with yours: a gift of story and song—soft, stirring melody in an ill-harmonized and unmelodious land; the gift of sweat and brawn to beat back the wilderness, conquer the soil, lay the foundations of the vast economic empire two hundred years before your weak hands could have done it; the third a gift of the spirit. . . . Our song, our toil, our cheer. . . . Would America have been America without her Negro people?"

I ask today: What future can America have without the free and unfettered contributions of our sixteen millions? What place of honor can our country have in the new world a-borning if our heritage is still denied?

I speak as an American Negro whose life is dedicated, first and foremost, to winning full freedom, and nothing less than full freedom, for my people in America. In these pages I have discussed what this fight for Negro freedom means in the crisis of today, of how it represents the decisive front in the struggle for democracy in our country, of how it relates to the cause of peace and liberation throughout the world. In presenting my views on this subject—and in one way or another all of America and much of the rest of the world is discussing it—I have sought to explain how I came to my viewpoint and to take the stand I have taken. As with other men, my views, my work, my life are all of one piece; for, as Frederick Douglass in his deep wisdom put it: "A man is worked on by what he works on. He may carve out his circumstances, but his circumstances will carve him out as well."

At the outset let me make one thing very clear: I care nothing—less than nothing—about what the lords of the land, the Big White Folks, think of me and my ideas. For more than ten years they have persecuted me in every way they could—by slander and mob violence, by denying me the right to practice my profession as an artist, by withholding my right to travel abroad. To these, the real Un-Americans, I merely say: "All right—I don't like *you* either!"

But I do care—and deeply—about the America of the common people whom I have met across the land . . . the working men and women whose picket-lines I've joined, auto workers, seamen, cooks and stewards, furriers, miners, steel workers; and the foreign-born, the various nationality groups, the Jewish people with whom I have been especially close; and the middle-class progressives, the people of the arts and sciences, the students—all of that America of which I sang in the *Ballad for Americans*, "the Etceteras and the And-so-forths, that do the work."

Most of all I am mindful of the Negro people and the questions they ask of me as I meet them in the Harlems of America. Inevitably—since in these last years I have been the center of much controversy—many of those questions deal with my views and activities. I think of the reporter on the *Pittsburgh Courier* who made an honest effort to find answers to the questions in the title of his article—"Who, What and Why is Paul Robeson?"—and who wrote that the picture was "complicated somewhat by the fact that Mr. Robeson has, in the minds of large numbers of Americans, two distinct personalities. One is that of the militant advocate of racial equality and human rights, and the other is that of an affectionate apostle of Soviet Communism." And then there was the *Afro-American* writer who concluded a similar study with these words: "If there is a mystery about Paul Robeson it is this. By singing spirituals he can be popular and wealthy; by fighting for his race he becomes despised and doors are closed against him. For the answer as to why he made this choice you will have to search the deep recesses of his soul."

Here and there, over the years, in various articles and interviews, I have tried to explain one or another facet of my life and thinking. But these hasty snatches and fragments are not enough, and so in these pages I have sought to tell the story more fully. In doing this, I have been assisted by my friend, the gifted Negro writer Lloyd L. Brown, and I am deeply grateful for the warm understanding and creative quality of his work with me. Though this book is not an autobiography, I thought it might be helpful at the outset to sketch briefly my early days and the lasting influences from my childhood. Let that story be here, as it was in life, a prologue to the chapters that follow.

PAUL ROBESON

New York
November, 1957

Prologue

A HOME IN THAT ROCK

THE GLORY OF MY BOYHOOD years was my father. I loved him like no one in all the world. His people, among whom he moved as a patriarch for many years before I was born, loved him, too. And the white folks—even the most lordly of aristocratic Princeton—had to respect him.

Born a plantation slave in Martin County, North Carolina, my father escaped at the age of fifteen, in 1860, and made his way North on the Underground Railroad. In 1876, after working his way through Lincoln University, he married my mother, Maria Louisa Bustill, a school teacher in nearby Philadelphia. Following a brief pastorate in Wilkes-Barre, Pennsylvania, he was called to be pastor of the Witherspoon Street Presbyterian Church in Princeton, New Jersey, where I was born on April 9, 1898.

I was the youngest of Reverend Robeson's children, and there were four others living at the time of my birth: William D., Jr., age 17; Reeve, 12; Benjamin, 6; and Marian, my only sister, who was 4.

In later years my father was pastor of A.M.E. Zion churches in the nearby towns of Westfield and Somerville, until his death in 1918, at the age of seventy-three. An editorial in the Somerville newspaper made this comment at the time:

> "The death of Rev. W. D. Robeson takes from this community one who has done a quiet but successful work among his own people for the past eight years. Mr. Robeson was a man of strong character . . . he was very familiar with the characteristics of his race and was always interested in their welfare. He quickly resented any attempt to belittle them or to interfere with their rights. He had

the temperament which has produced so many orators in the South and he held his people together in the church here with a fine discernment of their needs. He has left his impress on the colored race throughout the State and he will be greatly missed here."

Go today to the towns in that part of New Jersey and you will find his memory still warm in the communities he served. As you drive down on the highway past New Brunswick you may see the William D. Robeson Houses, a government project named for him. In Princeton, the Witherspoon Street Presbyterian Church still stands, with one of the stained-glass windows glowing "In Loving Remembrance of Sabra Robeson" who was my father's slave mother on the Carolina plantation. Many of the older church members and other long-time residents you might meet on the shady lanes of the Negro community nearby—Green Street, Hulfish Street, Quarry, Jackson, Birch, John—will tell you with quiet pride of my father's devoted labors, his wisdom, his dignity. And they will tell you, too, about my mother, Maria Louisa: how she moved, so strong and tender, in their midst—comforting the sick, mothering the orphaned, collecting food and clothing for the hungry and ragged, opening to many the wonders of book learning.

I cannot say that I remember her, though my memory of other things goes back before her tragic death. I was six years old when she, a near-blind invalid at the time, was fatally burned in a household accident. I remember her lying in the coffin, and the funeral, and the relatives who came, but it must be that the pain and shock of her death blotted out all other personal recollections. Others have told me of her remarkable intellect, her strength of character and spirit which contributed so much to my father's development and work. She was a companion to him in his studies; she helped compose his sermons; she was his right hand in all his community work.

Maria Louisa Robeson, born on November 8, 1853, in Philadelphia, was a member of the noted Bustill family. The history of the Bustills, who are of mixed Negro, Indian and white Quaker stock, goes back to the earliest days of America. My great-great-grandfather, Cyrus Bustill, who baked bread for Washington's troops, became a leader of the Negroes in Philadelphia; and in 1787 he was a founder of the Free African Society, first mutual aid organization of American Negroes. Through the years the Bustills produced many teachers, artists and scholars, and, in the Quaker tradition, took part in running the Underground Railroad by which so many, like my father, escaped from bondage.

I don't know if the custom is still observed, but when I was a boy the Bustill Family Association held annual reunions to which all of the relatives from far and near would come. I find in my college scrapbook a printed program of the reunion of 1918, held at Maple Grove in Philadelphia. My aunt, Gertrude Bustill Mossell, is listed as vice-president of the association; and on the program of the day was a reading of the family history by my cousin, Annie Bustill Smith, and speeches by various other members, including an address by "Mr. Paul Roberson." (Though this spelling of my name was a printer's error, it is likely that "Roberson" was the ancestral name of the slave-holding Robesons from whom my father got his name. The county seat of his birthplace, Martin County, N. C., is Robersonville; and one of the earliest Negro freedom petitions on record is that of a slave, Ned Griffin, who, in 1784, from Edgecombe County which adjoins Martin County, urged the state government to grant him the freedom that was promised for his services in the Revolutionary Army and which was being denied him by his owner, one Abner *Roberson*.)

I cannot recall anything I said in my speech on that occasion, though I did jot down in my scrapbook its title—"Loyalty to Convictions." That I chose this topic was not accidental, for that was the text of my father's life—loyalty to one's convictions. Unbending. Despite anything. From my youngest days I was imbued with that concept. This bedrock idea of integrity was taught by Reverend Robeson to his children not so much by preachment (for by nature Pop was re-strained of speech, often silent at home, and among us Robe-sons the deepest feelings are largely unexpressed in words) but, rather, by the daily example of his life and work.

Though my father was a man of ordinary height, he was very broad of shoulder and his physical bearing reflected the rock-like strength and dignity of his character. He had the greatest speaking voice I have ever heard. It was a deep, sonorous basso, richly melodic and refined, vibrant with the love and compassion which filled him. How proudly, as a boy, I walked at his side, my hand in his, as he moved among the people! There was a wide gap in years between us—he was fifty-three when I was born, near sixty when my mother died —but during many of his years as a widower I was the only child at home and his devoted care and attention bound us closely together. It was not like him to be demonstrative in his love, nor was he quick to praise. Doing the right thing —well, that was something to be taken for granted in his children. I knew what I must do—when to come home from play, my duties in the household, my time for study—and I readily yielded to his quiet discipline. Only once did I disobey him.

I was ten years old at the time, and we were then living in Westfield. My father told me to do something and I didn't do it. "Come here," he said; but I ran away. He ran after me. I darted across the road. He followed, stumbled and fell. I was horrified. I hurried back, helped Pop to his feet. He had knocked out one of his teeth. I have never forgotten the emo-tions—the sense of horror, shame, ingratitude, selfishness—that overwhelmed me. I adored him, would have given my life for him in a flash—and here I had hurt him, disobeyed him! Never did he have to admonish me again; and this incident became a source of tremendous discipline which has lasted through the years.

I have said that the white families who dominated Prince-ton recognized my father's dignity and accorded him re-spect. How remarkable that was, and what a tribute to his character, can be appreciated fully only when one recalls that the Princeton of my boyhood (and I don't think it has changed much since then) was for all the world like any small town in the deep South. Less than fifty miles from New York, and even closer to Philadelphia, Princeton was spiritually located in Dixie. Traditionally the great university—which is practically all there is in the town—has drawn a large part of its student body and faculty from below the Mason-Dixon Line, and along with these sons of the Bourbons came the most rigid social and economic patterns of White Supremacy. And like the South to which its heart belonged, Princeton's controlling mind was in Wall Street. Bourbon and Banker were one in Princeton, and there the decaying smell of the plantation Big House was blended with the crisper smell of the Countinghouse. The theology was Calvin: the religion—cash.

Rich Princeton was white: the Negroes were there to do the work. An aristocracy must have its retainers, and so the people of our small Negro community were, for the most part, a servant class—domestics in the homes of the wealthy, serving as cooks, waiters and caretakers at the university, coachmen for the town and laborers at the nearby farms and brickyards. I had the closest of ties with these workers since many of my father's relatives—Uncle Ben and Uncle John and Cousin Carraway and Cousin Chance and others—had come to this town and found employment at such jobs.

Princeton was Jim Crow: the grade school that I attended was segregated and Negroes were not permitted in any high school. My oldest brother, Bill, had to travel to Trenton—eleven miles away—to attend high school, and I would have had to do the same had we not moved to another town. No Negro students were admitted to the university, although one or two were allowed to attend the divinity school.

Under the caste system in Princeton the Negro, restricted to menial jobs at low pay and lacking any semblance of political rights or bargaining power, could hope not for justice but for charity. The stern hearts and tight purses of the master class could on occasion be opened by appeals from the "deserving poor," and then philanthropy, in the form of donations, small loans or cast-off clothing might be looked for. The Negro church, center of community life, was the main avenue through which such boons were sought and received, and, in fact, the Witherspoon Street Presbyterian Church was itself largely built by white philanthropy. The pastor was a sort of bridge between the Have-nots and the Haves, and he served his flock in many worldly ways—seeking work for the jobless, money for the needy, mercy from the Law.

In performing these Christian duties my father came to know and be known by all of the so-called "Best People" of the town. But though the door of the university president might be open to him, Reverend Robeson could not push open the doors of that school for his son, when Bill was ready for college. The pious president, a fellow Presbyterian, said: No, it is quite impossible. That was Woodrow Wilson—Virginian, graduate of Princeton, professor there for a decade, college president from 1902 to 1910, then Governor of New Jersey, elected President of the United States in 1912, re-elected in 1916 because "he kept us out of the war" into which he led the nation one month after his second inaugural, Nobel Peace Prize winner, apostle of the New Liberalism, advocate of democracy for the world and Jim Crow for America!

He who comes hat-in-hand is expected to bow and bend, and so I marvel that there was no hint of servility in my father's make-up. Just as in youth he had refused to remain a slave, so in all the years of his manhood he disdained to be an Uncle Tom. From him we learned, and never doubted it, that the Negro was in every way the equal of the white man. And we fiercely resolved to prove it.

That a so-called lowly station in life was no bar to a man's assertion of his full human dignity was heroically demonstrated by my father in the face of a grievous blow that came to him when I was still a baby. After more than two decades of honored leadership in his church, a factional dispute among the members removed him as pastor. Adding to the pain was the fact that some of his closest kin were part of the ousting faction. A gentle scholar and teacher all his adult life, my father, then past middle age, with an invalid wife and dependent children at home, was forced to begin life anew. He got a horse and a wagon, and began to earn his living hauling ashes for the townsfolk. This was his work at the time I first remember him and I recall the growing mound of dusty ashes dumped into our backyard at 13 Green Street. A fond memory remains of our horse, a mare named Bess, whom I grew to love and who loved me. My father also went into the hack business, and as a coachman drove the gay young students around town and on trips to the seashore.

Ash-man, coachman, he was still the dignified Reverend Robeson to the community, and no man carried himself with greater pride. Not once did I hear him complain of the poverty and misfortune of those years. Not one word of bitterness ever came from him. Serene, undaunted, he struggled to earn a livelihood and see to our education. Soon after the tragedy that took his wife from him, Pop sent my brother Ben away to prep school and Biddle University (now Johnson C. Smith) in North Carolina, and my sister Marian to Scotia Seminary, a school for colored girls in the same state. Bill, the oldest, was then at Lincoln University—the school my father had attended—and for a time Reeve (or Reed, as we called him) was at home, working as a hack driver.

Some might say that Reed did not turn out as well as the other Robeson children, and it is a fact that my father was sorely disappointed in this son and disapproved of his carefree and undisciplined ways. Yet I admired this rough older brother and I learned from him a quick militancy against racial insults and abuse. Many was the time that Reed, resenting some remark by a Southern gentleman-student, would leap down from his coachman's seat, drag out the offender and punish him with his fists. He always carried for protection a bag of small, jagged rocks—a weapon he used with reckless abandon whenever the occasion called for action.

Inevitably there were brushes with the Law, and then

my father, troubled in heart, would don his grave frock-coat
and go down to get Reed out of trouble again. But this happened once too often, and one day I stood sadly and silently
by as Pop told Reed he would have to leave—he must live
his life elsewhere because his example was a dangerous one
for his young brother Paul.

Reed is dead now. He won no honors in classroom, pulpit
or platform. Yet I remember him with love. Restless, rebel-
lious, scoffing at conventions, defiant of the white man's law
—I've known many Negroes like Reed. I see them every day.
Blindly, in their own reckless manner, they seek a way out
for themselves; alone, they pound with their fists and fury
against walls that only the shoulders of the many can topple.
"Don't ever take low," was the lesson Reed taught me. "Stand
up to them and hit back harder than they hit you!" When
the many have learned that lesson, everything will be different and then the fiery ones like Reed will be able to live
out their lives in peace and no one will have cause to frown
on them.

Because I was younger, my own days in Princeton were
happier ones. Mostly I played. There were the vacant lots
for ball games, and the wonderful moments when Bill, vaca-
tioning from college where he played on the team, would
teach me how to play football. He was my first coach, and
over and over again on a weed-grown lot he would put me
through the paces—how to tackle a man so he stayed tackled,
how to run with the ball. Then there were the winter evenings at home with Pop: he loved to play checkers and so
we two would sit for hours in the parlor, engrossed in our
game, not speaking much but wonderfully happy together.

My father never talked with us about his early years as
a slave or about his parents, Benjamin and Sabra, though
long afterward I learned from others that before his mother
died, Pop made at least one, and possibly two, dangerous
trips back to the plantation to see her. I'm sure that had he
ever spoken about this part of his life it would have been
utterly impossible for me as a boy to grasp the idea that a

noble human being like my father had actually been owned by another man—to be bought and sold, used and abused at will.

(I might mention here, in passing, that many years later in New York I met one of the family that had held my father in bondage. I had gone to a downtown night club to hear a friend who was singing in the place, and there I was accosted by a man who introduced himself as one of the Robesons of North Carolina. He said he was sure that I'd be pleased to hear that his mother was quite proud of my accomplishments in life, and that she had carefully kept a scrapbook on the various honors that I had won for the family name. Then the stranger went on to say that he would like to get together with me for a chat some day soon. "You see," he confided proudly, "your father used to work for my grandfather." As politely as was possible under the circumstances I assured the Southern gentleman that it was undoubtedly true that the Negroes who had come by his family's name had added a bit more distinction to it than did any of the original owners or their descendants. "You say my father 'used to work' for your grandfather. Let's put it the way it was: *Your grandfather exploited my father as a slave!*"—That ended it; and *this* Robeson never did have a chummy get-together with *that* one.)

Not old enough to work for them, I had very little connection with the white people of Princeton; but there were some white children among my playmates. One of these was a boy, about my age, whose father owned the neighborhood grocery a few doors from our house. We could not go to school together, of course, but during the long summer days we were inseparable companions at play. Once—and I don't remember why—the two of us got into a small-boy fight. After much crouching and circling and menacing gestures, we each got up enough courage to land a blow on the other's nose and then, wailing loudly, we ran away to our homes. Next day we were friends again.

There must have been moments when I felt the sorrows

of a motherless child, but what I most remember from my youngest days was an abiding sense of comfort and security. I got plenty of mothering, not only from Pop and my brothers and sister when they were home, but from the whole of our close-knit community. Across the street and down each block were all my aunts and uncles and cousins—including some who were not actual relatives at all. So, if I were to try to put down the names of all the folks who helped raise me, it would read like a roster of Negro Princeton. In a way I was "adopted" by all these good people, and there was always a place at their tables and a place in a bed (often with two or three other young ones) for Reverend Robeson's boy when my father was away on one of his trips to the seashore or attending a church conference.

Hard-working people, and poor, most of them, in worldly goods—but how rich in compassion! How filled with the goodness of humanity and the spiritual steel forged by centuries of oppression! There was the honest joy of laughter in these homes, folk-wit and story, hearty appetites for life as for the nourishing greens and black-eyed peas and cornmeal bread they shared with me. Here in this little hemmed-in world where home must be theatre and concert hall and social center, there was a warmth of song. Songs of love and longing, songs of trials and triumphs, deep-flowing rivers and rollicking brooks, hymn-song and ragtime ballad, gospels and blues, and the healing comfort to be found in the illimitable sorrow of the spirituals.

Yes, I heard my people singing!—in the glow of parlor coal-stove and on summer porches sweet with lilac air, from choir loft and Sunday morning pews—and my soul was filled with their harmonies. Then, too, I heard these songs in the very sermons of my father, for in the Negro's speech there is much of the phrasing and rhythms of folk-song. The great, soaring gospels we love are merely sermons that are sung; and as we thrill to such gifted gospel singers as Mahalia Jackson, we hear the rhythmic eloquence of our preachers, so many of whom, like my father, are masters of poetic speech.

There was something else, too, that I remember from Princeton. Something strange, perhaps, and not easy to describe. I early became conscious—I don't quite know how—of a special feeling of the Negro community for me. I was no different from the other kids of the neighborhood—playing our games of Follow the Leader and Run Sheep Run, saying "yes ma'am" and never sassing our elders, fearing to cross the nearby cemetery because of the "ghosts," coming reluctant and new-scrubbed to Sunday School. And yet, like my father, the people claimed to see something special about me. Whatever it was, and no one really said, they felt I was fated for great things to come. Somehow they were sure of it, and because of that belief they added an extra measure to the affection they lavished on their preacher's motherless child.

I didn't know what I was supposed to be when I grew up. A minister like my father? A teacher like my mother? Maybe. But whatever the vocation might be, I must grow up to be a "credit to the race," as they said. "You got something, boy, something deep down inside, that will take you to the top. You'll see—sure as I'm sitting here!" I wondered at times about this notion that I was some kind of child of destiny and that my future would be linked with the longed-for better days to come, but I didn't worry about it. Being grown up was a million years ahead. Now was the time for play.

Though we moved away from Princeton in 1907, when I was nine, I was back and forth between the other towns and this community until I finished college at twenty-one. Visiting Princeton was always being at home.

Westfield, where we moved first, was thirty-odd miles away in the direction of New York. For years in Princeton, after he lost his church, friends had told my father that he must return to preaching. And so, at the age of sixty-two, when he got the chance, he eagerly set out to begin all over again. Now he joined a different denomination, the African Methodist Episcopal Zion church. The Negro community of Westfield was even smaller than in Princeton and there were at the start not more than a dozen members in Reverend Robeson's new congregation to help him dig the foundation for the Downing Street A.M.E. Zion Church. There were too few Negro children for the town to have a separate school "for colored only," so the grade school I attended during the three years we lived there was mixed.

Westfield, and later Somerville, were quite unlike Princeton. Barriers between Negro and white existed, of course, but they were not so rigid; and in the ordinary way of small-town life there were more friendly connections between the two groups. And here there were white workingmen, too, many of them foreign-born, who, unlike the Princeton blue-bloods, could see in a workingman of a darker skin a fellow human being (a lower-paid worker, of course, and perhaps a competitor for a job, but not a person of a totally different caste).

In these towns I came to know more white people. I frequently visited the homes of my schoolmates and always received a friendly welcome. I wasn't conscious of it at the time, but now I realize that my easy moving between the two racial communities was rather exceptional. For one thing, I was the respected preacher's son, and then, too, I was popular with the other boys and girls because of my skill at sports and studies, and because I was always ready to share in their larks and fun-making. Observing my manner of respectful politeness and courtesy, in which Pop had trained us, some of the white parents encouraged their children's friendship with me, hoping, I suppose, that I might have a favorable influence on them. A good boy studied hard, helped with the chores, gladly ran errands, tipped his hat to ladies, always said "No thank you" when offered a piece of cake (at the first offer, that is), never puffed a cigarette or said bad words, would never in all his years touch a drop of hard liquor, never told lies, never played hookey, never missed Sunday School, and got nothing but A's on his report card.

Well, I was a good boy, sure enough—but I wasn't *that* good! Not all the time, at any rate. For my father gave my teachers permission to paddle me for any waywardness, and though I don't recall the misdeeds, this permission was firmly (and memorably) exercised on a couple of occasions.

In 1910 we moved to Somerville, a larger town midway between Westfield and Princeton, where Reverend Robeson served as pastor of St. Thomas A.M.E. Zion Church until his death eight years later. I attended eighth grade in Somerville (here again the school was all colored) and graduated at the head of my class. Pop was pleased by that, I guess, though it was only what he expected of me and his attitude never allowed for feelings of exaggerated self-esteem.

I have often told how he was never satisfied with a school mark of 95 when 100 was possible. But this was not because he made a fetish of perfection. Rather it was that the concept of *personal integrity,* which was his ruling passion, included inseparably the idea of *maximum human fulfillment.* Success in life was not to be measured in terms of money and personal advancement, but rather the goal must be the richest and highest development of one's own potential.

A love for learning, a ceaseless quest for truth in all its fullness—this my father taught. His own schooling had been along the classic pattern which today has been largely displaced by an emphasis on technology. I do not know, in political terms, what stand my father took in the debate then raging in Negro life between the militant policy of W. E. B. Du Bois and the conservative preachments of Booker T. Washington—that clash of opposing ideas as to the path for Negro progress which was so largely expressed in terms of educational goals. But in practice Reverend Robeson flatly rejected Washington's concept that Negro education be limited essentially to manual training; he firmly believed that the heights of knowledge must be scaled by the freedom-seeker. Latin, Greek, philosophy, history, literature—all the treasures of learning must be the Negro's heritage as well.

So for me in high school there would be four years of Latin and then in college four more years of Latin and Greek. Closely my father watched my studies, and was with me page by page through Virgil and Homer and the other classics in which he was well grounded. He was my first teacher in public speaking, and long before my days as class orator and college debater there were the evenings of recitations at home, where his love for the eloquent and meaningful word and his insistence on purity of diction made their impress.

High school in Somerville was not Jim Crow, and there I formed close friendships with a number of white classmates. One of these was Douglas Brown, a brilliant student who was in my class through the four years and who later became the dean of Princeton University. I was welcomed as a member of the glee club (unlike later at college) and the dramatic club and into the various sports and social activities around the school. The teachers also were friendly and several of them are especially remembered.

Miss Vosseller, the music teacher who directed our glee club, took a special interest in training my voice. Anna Miller, English teacher, paid close attention to my development as a speaker and debater; and it was she who first introduced me to Shakespeare's works. Many years were to pass before the American theatre would permit a Negro to play Othello, but the idea seemed eminently right to Miss Miller and she coached me in the part for a high-school dramatic performance. Nervous and scared, I struggled through the lines on that solemn occasion (mindful of my father's ear for perfect diction and my teacher's patient direction) and no one in the world could have convinced me then that I should ever try acting again.

Miss Vandeveer, who taught Latin, seemed to have no taint of racial prejudice; and Miss Bagg, instructor in chemistry and physics, made every effort to make me feel welcome and at ease in the school's social life of which she was in charge. Miss Bagg urged me to attend the various parties and dances, and when I did so, it was she who was the first to dance with me. But despite her encouragement, I shied away from most of these social affairs. There was always the feeling that—well, something unpleasant might happen; for the two worlds of white and Negro were nowhere more separate than in social life. Though I might visit the homes of white classmates, I was always conscious that I belonged to the Negro community.

From an early age I had come to accept and follow a certain protective tactic of Negro life in America, and I did not fully break with the pattern until many years later. Even while demonstrating that he is really an equal (and, strangely, the proof must be *superior* performance!) the Negro must never appear to be challenging white superiority. Climb up if you can—but don't act "uppity." Always show that you are *grateful*. (Even if what you have gained has been wrested from unwilling powers, be sure to be grateful lest "they" take it all away.) Above all, *do nothing to give them cause to fear you*, for then the oppressing hand, which might at times ease up a little, will surely become a fist to knock you down again!

Well, as a boy in high school I tried my best to "act right." I would make the best of my opportunities. I would measure myself only against my own potential and not see myself in competition with anyone else. Certainly I had no idea of challenging the way things were. But courtesy and restraint did not shield me from all hostility: it soon became clear that the high school principal hated me. Dr. Ackerman, who later rose to higher positions in the New Jersey school system, made no effort to hide his bitter feelings. The better I did, the worse his scorn. The cheers of my fellow students as I played fullback on the football team—"Let Paul carry the ball! Yay—Paul!"—seemed to curdle the very soul of Dr. Ackerman; and when the music teacher made me soloist of the glee club it was against the principal's furious opposition.

He never spoke to me except to administer a reprimand; and he seemed constantly to be looking for an excuse to do so. One fault I had was occasionally being late to class in the morning—probably because our house was only a few hundred yards from the school! "Early to bed and early to rise" was always a hard rule for me to keep, and sometimes I misjudged the few minutes needed to get up and get to class. Then, like a watchful hawk, Dr. Ackerman would pounce on me, and his sharp words were meant to make me feel as miserably inferior

as he thought a Negro was. One time he sent me home for punishment. Usually Pop preferred that the teacher's hand rather
than his own should administer the proper penalty, but this
time I had something to say about that. "Listen, Pop," I said,
"I'm bigger now. I don't care what *you* do to me, but if that
hateful old principal ever lays a hand on me, I swear I'll try
my best to break his neck!" I guess Pop understood. He let it
go at that.

Of lasting value during these formative years was the devoted help of my brothers and sister in the periods when they
were at home.*

There was Bill, the oldest, to whom the other children of
Reverend Robeson gave first place as far as "brains" were
concerned. Though I have met many other brilliant persons
in the years since then, time has not lessened the marveling
regard I had for Bill's mental powers. Like Reed, he is dead;
and his potential was never fulfilled. He seemed always to be
going to school—at Lincoln and Penn, in Boston and at Howard—except for interludes when his money was exhausted
and he went to work at such jobs as were open to Negroes.
At various times he got work "running on the road" as a Pull-
man porter, and for a while he was a redcap at Grand Central Station in New York where his fellows, impressed by his
erudition, bestowed on him the nickname "Deep Stuff."

More formal recognition of his scholarship came to Bill:
his field was medicine and he earned his degree. But by temperament Bill was not meant to be a practicing physician.
I'm sure that if faced with the workaday task of setting a
broken bone, Bill's mind would be concentrating on Lord
knows what. (Maybe on the history of bone-setting going
back to the ancient Egyptians, or wondering about the molec-
ular structure of bones in general—or, more likely, grappling
with some problem of medical theory not even remotely related to the job at hand.) Bill should have found a place in
some scientific laboratory where his restless, searching mind

* See Appendix A, page 112.

might have been applied to the finding of deep-hidden answers (with someone else around to see to it that some test tubes were at hand and to jot down a finding before Bill forgot about it in his zest for discovering something else.)

Though his gift for theory and analysis had such little practical effect on his own life, for me Bill was the principal source of learning how to study. During my high school years in Somerville, Bill was often at home, between colleges and railroad runs, and he spent much time directing my studies. He was never satisfied when I came up with a correct answer. "Yes, but *why?*" he would insist sharply. What was the relation of one fact to another? What was the system, the framework, of a given study? When I couldn't explain, Bill would quickly and clearly demonstrate the mystery to me; and to my constant amazement he could do that, after a very short inquiry, even in subjects he himself had not previously studied. Often nowadays, when I am struggling with some difficult question in language or music study, trying to "break down" the particular system involved, I think of this brother and tutor and say to myself: "I'll bet if Bill were here he'd lick this problem in no time!"

It was my brother Ben who most inspired my interest in sports. Ben was an outstanding athlete by any standards, and had he attended one of the prominent colleges I'm convinced he would have been chosen All-American. Certainly he ranked in ability with many of the famous stars I later encountered in college games and professional football. Ben was also a remarkable baseball player, fleet of foot and a power at bat; and had Negroes then been permitted to play in the major leagues, I think that Ben was one of those who could have made the grade.

Closer to me in age than my other brothers, Ben was my favorite. It was he who first took me out into the world beyond our small-town life. When I was about fourteen, and in high school, Ben got a job for the summer as a waiter at Narragansett Pier, in Rhode Island, where many Negro students found vacation-time employment in the resorts of the

rich. I went along with Ben, to serve as kitchen boy. My work
—and I'm sure I have never again in all my life worked quite
so hard—began at 4:00 A.M. and it was late evening before
I emerged from the mountains of pots and pans I scrubbed,
the potatoes I peeled, the endless tasks ordered by the
chef, the second cooks and helpers, all of whom outranked
the kitchen boy and who were finished long before he had
mopped up for the last time and put everything away in
gleaming splendor. But always there was the comforting
presence of brother Ben, around somewhere, keeping a watchful eye out for the kid brother in the kitchen who was be-
wildered by the rush and clatter of his first job, innocent
among the other, more worldly-wise, workers. Later, in college
days, I would go back again to Narragansett, and there,
among the waiters, bus boys and kitchen help, I made many
friendships which last until today. From among these student-
workers came many of the leading Negro professionals whom
I meet around the country today.

My sister Marion was not at home as much as Ben, but the
thought of Sis always brings an inner smile. She lives now
in Philadelphia, with her husband, Dr. William Forsythe.
'If it turned out that it was to be Ben who followed my father's
calling as a minister, it was Marion who continued the teach-
ing traditions of my mother's family. As a girl she brought to
our household the blessing of laughter, so filled is she with
warm good humor. When she was at home from school, Sis
did the cooking, but firmly believing that a woman's place
was not in anybody's kitchen—at least not for long—she always left the big stack of dishes . . . for me! (We laugh
about that, too, when we get together.)

With all her happy ways, Marion was earnestly resolved
to stand on her own feet and make a way for herself, aware,
more keenly than the rest of us, of the double burden that
a Negro woman bears in striving for dignity and fulfillment
in our boasted "way of life." As a young woman she became
a school teacher in Philadelphia and remained in that vocation until recently. I recall with pride her dedication to work

with so-called backward children, and her zeal to prove that devoted attention can bring these along with all others.

Marion and Ben—the two of them so much like my father in temperament. Reserved of speech, strong in character, living up to their principles—and always selflessly devoted to their youngest brother who cannot express in words his gratitude for their love. But in his heart there is a song, the most tender of songs—for them!

When I was seventeen and in my final semester at high school, I still had no vocation in mind. Singer? No, that was just for fun. Dramatics? Not I! There was the lingering thought, never too definite, of studying for the ministry; and though my father would have liked that choice, he never pressed it upon me. Perhaps in college I'd come to a decision about a career. The choice of a college had long been settled —Lincoln University, of which Pop and Bill were alumni.

But then, in my senior year at Somerville High, I learned about a competitive examination open to all students in New Jersey; the prize—a four-year scholarship to Rutgers College. Now a state university with an enrollment of over 12,000, Rutgers was then a private school with fewer than a thousand students. I knew about the college, for it was only fifteen miles away, in New Brunswick. One of the oldest colleges in America (founded in 1766), it was considered rather exclusive; and while one or two Negroes had once been admitted, none had attended Rutgers for many years.

Pop said I should take the examination, which for our county would be held in the Somerville Courthouse. Lincoln was our preference, but if I managed to win this scholarship the financial strain on my father's modest income would be eased. There was one big hitch: I should have taken a preliminary test the previous year, covering the subjects studied in the first three years of high school. Somehow I had not known about it then, and so now I was faced with an examination embracing the entire four-year course, in the same three-hour period during which the other competitors would

cover only their senior year's work. Still, even with this handi-
cap, we decided the prize was worth trying for, and I set
to work getting ready for the big day. The extra hurdle
called for extraordinary effort, and I studied hard until late
at night. The good wishes of classmates and teachers and the
ill-will of Dr. Ackerman, the principal, were spurs; and, most
of all, Pop's quiet confidence had to be justified.

Well, I won the scholarship—and here was a decisive point
in my life. That I would go to Rutgers was the least of it,
for I was sure I'd be happier at Lincoln. The important thing
was this: *Deep in my heart from that day on was a conviction
which none of the Ackermans of America would ever be able
to shake.* Equality might be denied, but I *knew* I was not
inferior.

Soon after the scholarship examination, in the spring of
1915, I took part in a state-wide oratorical contest of high
school students that was held at Rutgers. Prize debater at
Somerville High, diligent student of my father's artistry of
speech, I shared the high hopes of my family and classmates
that I might win first place. I didn't. First prize was won by
Hilmar Jensen, a Negro student from Asbury Park (his father,
too, was a minister); second place went to a white girl; and
I was third.

The speech I declaimed on that occasion was Wendell
Phillips' famous oration on Toussaint L'Ouverture. I don't
know why I picked that material for the contest (I guess it
was my brother Bill's idea), but now I marvel at the selection
for I had no real appreciation of its meaning, nor did I have
any idea of the significance of a Negro reciting it to an
audience that was mostly white. But there I was, voicing, with
all the fervor and forensic skill I could muster, Wendell
Phillips' searing attack on the concept of white supremacy!
His eulogy of the great Haitian revolutionary was made in
New York and Boston during the first year of the Civil War,
before Emancipation, and he had challenged his audiences of
"blue-eyed Saxons, proud of your race," to show him *"the*

*man of Saxon lineage for whom his most sanguine admirers
will wreathe with a laurel such as embittered* foes *have placed
on the brow of this Negro!"*

Here was the fiery Toussaint speaking to the blacks whom
he had led in a victorious rebellion and against whom Napo-
leon was sending General Leclerc with 30,000 troops:

> *"My children, France comes to make us slaves. God
> gave us liberty; France has no right to take it away. Burn
> the cities, destroy the harvests, tear up the roads with
> cannon, poison the wells, show the white man the hell he
> comes to make!"*

(Strong meat for a babe! But I was concentrating on getting the phrasing and diction just right and gave no thought
to the meaning of the flaming words.)

True, there were softening touches in the speech where
Wendell Phillips assured the good white people listening to
him that Toussaint L'Ouverture had not only spared his former
master and mistress but had benevolently provided for their
future welfare, and that every one of his black generals had
been equally magnanimous with the household that had
owned him. ("Loud cheers" were indicated in the printed
record of Phillips' address and perhaps this thought was also
happily received by the audience that heard me.)

Yet relentlessly the Abolitionist orator had hammered away
at his theme: the Negro, still enslaved in the South and despised in the North, was in every respect the equal of the
white man; and that Toussaint, *"a pure-blooded African,"* was
not only the First of the Blacks, as he was known, but peer-
less among all men. And so I went through it all, to the great,
soaring climax—giving it all I had in voice and gesture:

> *"You think me a fanatic tonight, for you read history
> not with your eyes but with your prejudices. But . . . the
> Muse of History will put Phocion for the Greek, Brutus
> for the Roman, Hampden for England, Fayette for France,
> choose Washington as the bright, consummate flower of
> our earlier civilization, and John Brown the ripe flower
> of our noonday, then, dipping her pen in the sunlight,*

will write in the clear blue, above them all, the name of
the soldier, the statesman, the martyr—Toussaint L'Ouver-
ture!"

(If I ever enter another oratorical contest, I'd like to try
that one again.)

Wendell Phillips—the best kind of American! Fighter for
Negro liberation, white comrade of our great Frederick
Douglass, speaker in countless towns across the land—"on a
literary subject, fee one hundred dollars; if on slavery, free."
On that occasion I paid tribute only to his powers of rhetoric,
but I would come to learn, in my own way, the great truth
he spoke of when, after chattel slavery was abolished, he
joined the fight for Labor's emancipation: *"When I want to*
find the vanguard of the people I look to the uneasy dreams
of an aristocracy and find what they dread most."

I knew little of such matters that fall of 1915 when I entered college to learn more Latin and Greek, more Physics
and Math, more History which included neither Toussaint nor
Phillips—and to play a little more football, too. As I went
out into life, one thing loomed above all else: I was my
father's son, a Negro in America. That was the challenge.

In the pages which follow I do not tell the story of my life
since childhood, because that is not the purpose of this book.
Although many later personal experiences are related in the
succeeding chapters, I have sought to present my ideas about
a subject that is infinitely more important than any personal
story—the struggle of my people for freedom. All which came
later, after Rutgers and Columbia Law School—my career
as an artist in America and abroad, my participation in public
life, the views which I hold today—all have their roots in the
early years recalled in this prologue.

Chapter 1

I TAKE MY STAND

IN RECENT YEARS my political views—or what are alleged to be my political views—have been the subject of wide discussion and controversy in public life generally and in Negro life as well. So many others have had their say on this matter that it seems only fair that I should have a chance to speak for myself, and so at this point I shall deal directly with that subject. My purpose in doing so is not to advance any partisan argument, but to set the record straight. I shall try to make clear exactly what my ideas are and how I came to hold them.

At the outset, let me point out that the controversy concerning my views and actions had its origin not among the Negro pepole but among the white folks on top who have directed at me the thunderbolts of their displeasure and rage. Although at various times certain Negro voices were heard joining in the condemnation that came from on high, it has been quite evident that the Negro community has its own way of looking at the matter.

One reaction, expressed by a wide range of Negro opinion extending from the most conservative to the most radical, is a keen resentment against certain ideas of my white critics. When it was said (and it was said many times) that Paul Robeson had shown himself to be ungrateful to the good white folks of America who had given him wealth and fame, and that he had had nothing to complain about, the statement was bound to rub Negroes the wrong way. They know that nothing is ever "given" to us, and they know that human dignity cannot be measured in dollars and cents. The late

Walter White expressed this sentiment in an article in *Ebony*:

"No honest American, white or Negro, can sit in judgment on a man like Robeson unless and until he has
sacrificed time, talent, money and popularity in doing
the utmost to root out the racial and economic evils which
infuriate men like Robeson."

However, another common reaction in Negro life has been
considerable confusion as to why I said or did certain things
when the only result seemed to be increased difficulties for
me; and then, too, it has been felt that the fire directed at me
was putting many other Negroes "on the spot." I have often
been asked: "Paul, are you doing right by being so outspoken
in these times of hysteria?" And: "Wouldn't you be of greater
service to the race if you just devoted yourself to being an
artist and didn't make those speeches which get the white
folks so upset?" And: "Man, what did you really say over
there in Paris that caused such a fuss?"

I shall be glad to answer all such questions in these pages,
and from what is happening nowadays I think that people
will understand me better than would have been the case a
few years ago. Recently, when Louis Armstrong denounced
mistreatment of Negroes, and in stronger words than I have
ever chosen, and when the response from other Negroes
(including Jackie Robinson, as I was pleased to see) was a
fervent Amen!—well, it looked like the "Old Ark's a-movering"
for real!

It has been largely forgotten, and perhaps not known at
all to many younger people, that my basic views on world
affairs are nothing new. More than twenty years have passed
since I first visited the Soviet Union and voiced my friendly
sentiments about the peoples of that land, and before that
I had expressed a keen interest in the life and culture of the
African peoples and a deep concern for their liberation. Indeed, before the "cold war" brought about a different atmosphere, those broader interests of mine were considered
by many Negroes to be quite admirable; and when in 1944
I was honored by the National Association for the Advance-

ment of Colored People with the Spingarn Medal, my activities in behalf of "freedom for all men" were said to be a special contribution that I had made. The same point was made in 1943 when I was awarded an honorary degree by Morehouse College of Atlanta,* and no one on that occasion was at all disturbed when in my speech of acceptance I observed that "the tremendous strides of the various peoples in the Soviet Union have given greatest proof of the latent abilities, not only of so-called agricultural peoples presumably unfitted for intricate industrial techniques, but also of so-called backward peoples who have clearly demonstrated that they function like all others."

We know, of course, how drastically the political climate of our country changed in the postwar years, but even in the worst period of McCarthyism—which, happily, now seems to be passing—I saw no reason why my convictions should change with the weather. I was not raised that way, and neither the promise of gain nor the threat of loss has ever moved me from my firm convictions. I recall that in 1936, when I was in London, John Hamilton, then national chairman of the Republican Party, visited me with a proposition that I return to America and campaign among Negroes for Alf Landon against President Roosevelt. My reward would be that as an actor I could write my own ticket in regard to future Hollywood contracts and starring productions, since the big film magnates were staunchly Republican and hated the man in the White House. I declined the offer and today I can smile at the thought that anyone could imagine me stumping the country, urging Negroes to turn against the New Deal and return the party of Herbert Hoover to power! Much earlier in my career, in New York, I had declined the offer of an important impresario to sign me to a lucrative ten-year contract while he would take full charge of my public life. I did not have many fixed ideas in those days, but one

* See Appendix B, page 114.

of them happened to be a strong conviction that my own conscience should be my guide and that no one was going to
lead me around by a golden chain or any other kind.

In the early days of my career as an actor, I shared what
was then the prevailing attitude of Negro performers—that
the content and form of a play or film scenario was of little
or no importance to us. What mattered was the opportunity,
which came so seldom to our folks, of having a part—any part
—to play on the stage or in the movies; and for a Negro actor
to be offered a *starring* role—well, that was a rare stroke of
fortune indeed! Later I came to understand that the Negro
artist could not view the matter simply in terms of his individual interests, and that he had a responsibility to his
people who rightfully resented the traditional stereotyped por-
trayals of Negroes on stage and screen. So I made a decision: If the Hollywood and Broadway producers did not
choose to offer me worthy roles to play, then I would choose
not to accept any other kind of offer. When, during the war
years, I had the chance to appear before American audiences in a major Shakespearean production (fifteen years
after I had first done so in London), I was deeply gratified
to know that my people felt, as Dr. Benjamin Mays put it,
that I had "rendered the Negro race and the world a great
service in Othello by demonstrating that Negroes are capable
of great and enduring interpretations in the realm of the
theatre as over against the typical cheap performances that
Hollywood and Broadway too often insist on Negroes doing."

Progress has been made and today there are greater opportunities for Negro performers. But it is still a hard struggle to win an equal place for them in the theatre, films, radio
and television; and I am very happy and proud to see that
so many of our brilliant young actors, singers and dancers are
fighting for decent scripts, for roles that are worthy of their
artistic talents. Years ago when I refused to sing before a
segregated audience the story was headline news, and today
I am happy to note that many others also have taken that

stand, and that nowadays it is considered news—and bad news, by our people—whenever a prominent Negro artist agrees to perform under Jim Crow arrangements. We have every right to take great pride in the new and rising generation of our artists and we ought to support them in their struggle for equal opportunity. Their notable effort to represent faithfully our people in the arts makes such support a duty for us all.

It was in London, in the years that I lived among the people of the British Isles and traveled back and forth to many other lands, that my outlook on world affairs was formed. This fact is a key to an understanding of why I may differ in certain attitudes from many others of my generation in Negro life.

Having begun my career as a concert singer and actor in the United States, I first went abroad, like many other Negro performers, to work at my profession. If today the opportunities for Negro artists are still very limited in our country, it was many times worse thirty years ago. After several trips back and forth, I decided to stay in Europe and to make my home in London. My reasons were quite the same as those which over the years have brought millions of Negroes out of the Deep South to settle in other parts of the country. It must be said, however, that for me London was infinitely better than Chicago has been for Negroes from Mississippi.

Others have written about the success I achieved in the greater opportunities I found in England, but that is not my story here. I was, of course, deeply gratified to gain a prominent place in the theatre, in films, as concert singer and popular recording artist. Even more gratifying was the friendly welcome I received in English society. At first it was mostly "high society"—the upper-class people who patronized the arts and largely comprised the concert audiences; and I found myself moving a great deal in the most aristocratic circles. Here I was treated (in the old-fashioned phrase that still has meaning in England) as a gentleman and a scholar. My

background at Rutgers and my interest in academic studies
were given much more weight than such matters are given
in America where bankrolls count more than brains and where
bookish people are often derided as "eggheads" when they
are not suspected of being "subversive." And so I found
in London a congenial and stimulating intellectual atmosphere in which I felt at home. And, to an American Negro,
the marked respect for law and order which is common among
all classes throughout the British Isles was especially pleas-
ing. They simply would not put up with a Faubus over
there.

In those happy days, had someone suggested that my home
should be "back home" in Jim Crow America I would have
thought he was out of his mind.   Go *back*—well, what in
Heaven's name *for?* Later, when I changed my base in English life and found myself more at home among the common
people, I liked that country even better and, beyond an occasional trip to the States, I thought that I was settled for life.

But London was the center of the British Empire and it
was there that I "discovered" Africa. That discovery, which
has influenced my life ever since, made it clear that I would
not live out my life as an adopted Englishman, and I came
to consider that I was an African.

Like most of Africa's children in America, I had known
little about the land of our fathers, but in England I came
to know many Africans. Some of their names are now known
to the world—Nkrumah and Azikiwe, and Kenyatta who is
imprisoned in Kenya. Many of the Africans were students,
and I spent long hours talking with them and taking part in
their activities at the West African Students Union building.
Somehow they came to look upon me as one of them; they
took pride in my successes; and they made Mrs. Robeson and
me honorary members of the Union. Besides these students,
who were mostly of princely origin, I also came to know another class of Africans—the seamen in the ports of London,
Liverpool and Cardiff. They too had their organizations,

and had much to teach me about their lives and their various peoples.

As an artist it was natural that my first interest in Africa was cultural. Culture? The foreign rulers of that continent insisted that there was no culture worthy of the name in Africa. But already musicians and sculptors in Europe were astir with their discovery of African art. And as I plunged, with excited interest, into my studies of Africa at the London School of Oriental Languages, I came to see that African culture was indeed a treasure-store for the world. Those who scorned the African languages as so many "barbarous dialects" could never know, of course, the richness of those languages and of the great philosophy and epics of poetry that have come down through the ages in these ancient tongues.

I studied many of these African languages, as I do to this day: Yoruba, Efik, Twi, Ga and others. Here was something important, I felt, not only for me as a student but for my people at home, and I expressed that thought in an article, "The Culture of the Negro," published in *The Spectator* (June 15, 1934), from which I quote these lines:

"It is astonishing and, to me, fascinating to find a flexibility and subtlety in a language like Swahili, sufficient to convey the teachings of Confucius, for example, and it is my ambition to guide the Negro race by means of its own peculiar qualities to a higher degree of perfection along the lines of its natural development. Though it is a commonplace to anthropologists, these qualities and attainments of Negro languages are entirely unknown to the general public of the Western world and, astonishingly enough, even to Negroes themselves. I have met Negroes in the United States who believed that the African Negro communicated his thoughts by means of gestures, that, in fact, he was practically incapable of speech and merely used sign language!

"It is my first concern to dispel this regrettable and abysmal ignorance of the value of its own heritage in the Negro race itself. . . ."

I felt as one with my African friends and became filled with a glowing pride in these riches, new found to me. I learned that along with the towering achievements of the cultures of ancient Greece and China there stood the culture of Africa, unseen and denied by the imperialist looters of Africa's material wealth. I came to see the roots of my own people's culture, especially in our music which is still the richest and most healthy in America. Scholars had traced the influence of African music to Europe—to Spain with the Moors, to Persia and India and China, and westward to the Americas. And I came to learn of the remarkable kinship between African and Chinese culture (of which I hope to write at length some day).

My pride in Africa, and it grew with the learning, impelled me to speak out against the scorners. I wrote articles for the *New Statesman and Nation, The Spectator* and elsewhere championing the real but unknown glories of African culture. I argued and discussed the subject with men like H. G. Wells, and Laski, and Nehru; with students and savants.

Now, there was a logic to this cultural struggle I was making, and the powers-that-be realized it before I did. The British Intelligence came one day to caution me about the political meaning of my activities. For the question loomed of itself: *If African culture was what I insisted it was, what happens then to the claim that it would take 1,000 years for Africans to be capable of self-rule?*

It was an African who directed my interest in Africa to something he had observed in the Soviet Union. On a visit to that country he had traveled east and had seen the Yakuts, a people who had been classed as a "backward race" by the Czars. He had been struck by the resemblance between the tribal life of the Yakuts and his own people of East Africa. What would happen to a people like the Yakuts now that they had been freed from colonial oppression and were part of the construction of a socialist society?

Well, I went to see for myself and on my first visit to the Soviet Union in 1934 I saw how the Yakuts and the Uzbeks and all the other formerly oppressed nations were leaping ahead from tribalism to modern industrial economy, from illiteracy to the heights of knowledge. Their ancient cultures blooming in new and greater richness. Their young men and women mastering the sciences and arts. A thousand years? No. Less than twenty!

So, through my interest in Africa I came to visit and to study what was going on in the Soviet Union. I have told many times how pleased I was to find a place where colored people walked secure and free as equals. Others had observed that fact before I did and others have seen it since. Not long ago I read in the *Afro-American* a report by Dr. William E. Reed, dean of the school of agriculture at the Agricultural and Technical College in North Carolina, on his recent visit to the Soviet Union, in which he said:

> "I saw no signs of racial discrimination. I think it is fair to say that racial discrimination is non-existent in the U.S.S.R. . . . I saw no difference between the way colored and white people live in the U.S.S.R. They are not segregated anywhere; those who attend church worship in the same churches; they attend the same schools."

That's how it is. I can't imagine that any Negro would not be pleased to see it, and I certainly was. So I thought that it would be a good thing to send my boy to school in the Soviet Union, and he did attend public school there for two years. Much has been made of that simple fact, but Paul, Jr., who later went to high school in Springfield, Massachusetts, and graduated from Cornell in New York, says that the Moscow school was a wonderful experience, that he had good teachers and good playmates, that he learned the language well—and why should that disturb anybody? (Evidently it did disturb the State Department because that fact was cited as one of the reasons why I should be denied a passport!)

I came to believe that the experiences of the many peoples and races in the Soviet Union—a vast country which embraces one-sixth of the earth's surface—would be of great value for other peoples of the East in catching up with the modern world. Today, with so many of these peoples in Asia and Africa gaining their freedom, there are many among them, including outstanding leaders, who say that they find in the Soviet achievements and those of the new China much that is of value. In a country like India, for example, there is a widespread opinion that socialism, in one form or another, must be considered as a possible solution of their problems.

I felt, too, that the rapidly growing power of the Soviet Union in world affairs would become an important factor in aiding the colonial liberation movement; and when, not long ago, the world saw how vigorously and effectively the Soviet Union moved to block Western imperialism from retaking the Suez Canal from emancipated Egypt, the truth of this view seemed amply confirmed. Here in New York, at the United Nations, we have all been able to see with our own eyes that on every issue that has come up the Soviet Union and the other socialist countries have voted in support of the colored peoples of the world. Some people say this is merely a matter of playing politics, but wouldn't it be wonderful for colored people everywhere if the U.S. delegation to the U.N. also played politics by voting that way?

Asia and Africa are looking at world developments with their eyes wide open and they don't miss a thing. As the influential newspaper *West African Pilot* put it in an editorial (June 30, 1953):

"We know no more about Communism than what its American and British detractors have pushed across to us as propaganda. . . . But judging from what we see and experience from day to day, we feel that all this talk of the so-called 'free world' and 'iron curtain' is a camouflage to fool and bamboozle colonial peoples. It is part and parcel of power politics into which we refuse to be drawn until we are free to choose which ideology suits us best.

"For the time being, we shall judge every nation strictly on the merits of the attitude of that nation towards our national aspirations. We have every cause to be grateful to the Communists for their active interest in the fate of colonial peoples and for their constant denunciation of the evils of imperialism. It is then left to the so-called 'free' nations to convince us that they are more concerned about our welfare than the Communists, and in this regard we believe more in action than in mere words."

The Bible says "by their deeds shall ye know them," and the colored nations cannot go wrong by taking that ancient truth as their guide.

My views concerning the Soviet Union and my warm feelings of friendship for the peoples of that land, and the friendly sentiments which they have often expressed toward me, have been pictured as something quite sinister by Washington officials and other spokesmen for the dominant white group in our country. It has been alleged that I am part of some kind of "international conspiracy."

The truth is: *I am not and never have been involved in any international conspiracy or any other kind, and do not know anyone who is.* It should be plain to everybody—and especially to Negroes—that if the government officials had a shred of evidence to back up that charge, you can bet your last dollar that they would have tried their best to put me *under* their jail! But they have no such evidence, because that charge is a lie. By an arbitrary and, as I am insisting in the courts, *illegal* ruling they have refused me a passport. In a later chapter I shall discuss the issues involved in that case, but here let me say that the denial of my passport is proof of nothing except the State Department's high-handed disregard of civil liberties.

In 1946, at a legislative hearing in California, I testified under oath that I was not a member of the Communist Party, but since then I have refused to give testimony or to sign affidavits as to that fact. There is no mystery involved in this refusal. As the witchhunt developed, it became clear that an important issue of Constitutional rights was involved in the making of such inquiries, and the film writers and directors who became known as the Hollywood Ten challenged the right of any inquisitors to violate the First Amendment's provisions of free speech and conscience. They lost their fight in the courts and were imprisoned. but since then the Supreme Court has made more liberal rulings in similar cases. The fundamental issue, however, is still not resolved, and I have made it a matter of principle, as many others have done, to refuse to comply with any demand of legislative committees or departmental officials that infringes upon the Constitutional rights of all Americans.

On many occasions I have publicly expressed my belief in the principles of scientific socialism, my deep conviction that for all mankind a socialist society represents an advance to a higher stage of life—that it is a form of society which is economically, socially, culturally, and ethically superior to a system based upon production for private profit. History shows that the processes of social change have nothing in common with silly notions about "plots" and "conspiracies." The development of human society—from tribalism to feudalism, to capitalism, to socialism—is brought about by the needs and aspirations of mankind for a better life. Today we see that hundreds of millions of people—a majority of the world's population—are living in socialist countries or are moving in a socialist direction, and that newly emancipated nations of Asia and Africa are seriously considering the question as to which economic system is the better for them to adopt. Some of their most outstanding leaders argue that the best road to their peoples' goals is through a socialist development and they point to the advances made by the Soviet Union, the People's Republic of China and other socialist countries as proof of their contention.

I do not intend to argue here for my political viewpoint, and, indeed, the large question as to which society is better for humanity is never settled by argument. The proof of the pudding is in the eating. Let the various social systems compete with each other under conditions of peaceful coexistence, and the people can decide for themselves. I do not insist that anyone else must agree with my judgment, and so I feel that no one is justified in insisting that I must conform to his beliefs. Isn't that fair?

In the wide acquaintanceships that I have had over the years, I have never hesitated to associate with people who hold non-conformist or radical views, and this has been true since my earliest days in the American theatre where I first met people who challenged the traditional order of things. And so today, Benjamin J. Davis is a dear friend of mine and I have always been pleased to say so; and he has been for many years a leader of the Communist Party of this country. I have known Ben Davis for a long time: I admired him when, as a young lawyer in Atlanta, he bravely defended a framed-up Negro youth and eventually won the case; I admired him later when, as a City Councilman in New York, he championed the rights of our people; and I admired him when, during his imprisonment, he began a legal fight to break down the Jim Crow system in the Federal penitentiaries. How could I *not* feel friendly to a man like that?

I firmly believe that Ben Davis and his colleagues were unjustly convicted, as Justice Black and Justice Douglas insisted in their dissenting opinion; and I think that their dissent in that case will be upheld in the course of history, as was the lone dissent in 1896 of Justice Harlan in the *Plessy versus Ferguson* case which was reversed in 1954 by a unanimous Court decision that the infamous "separate but equal" doctrine was unconstitutional and that Jim Crow schools were therefore unlawful. Indeed, already in several other Smith Act cases convicted persons have been vindicated by higher court action. In one case that was appealed to a

Federal court, Judge William H. Hastie's forthright stand for civil liberties and against the convictions was a minority opinion; but since then, as a result of other decisions by that court and the U.S. Supreme Court, the Smith Act victims have been completely vindicated.

The main charge against me has centered upon my remarks at the World Peace Conference held in Paris in 1949, and what I said on that occasion has been distorted and misquoted in such a way as to impugn my character as a loyal American citizen. I went to Paris from England where, the night before I left, I met with the Coordinating Committee of Colonial Peoples in London, together with Dr. Y. M. Dadoo, president of the South African Indian Congress. The facts about that meeting and what I said in Paris are contained in the testimony I gave before the House Committee on Un-American Activities (a more accurate term is "Un-American Committee"!) at a hearing to which I was summoned on June 12, 1956. (This was *seven years* after another person, who was not in Paris and who did not know what I said there, was called before that Committee to give his views on what I was supposed to have said!)

Referring to the London meeting and my remarks next day in Paris, I testified as follows:

"It was 2,000 students from various parts of the colonial world, from populations that would range from six to 700 million people, not just fifteen million. They asked me to address this [Paris] Conference and say in their name that they did not want war. That is what I said. There is no part of my speech in Paris which says that fifteen million Negroes would do anything. . . . But what is perfectly clear today is that 900 million other colored people have told you they will not [go to war with the Soviet Union]. Is that not so? Four hundred million in India and millions everywhere have told you precisely that the colored people are not going to die for anybody and they are going to die for their independence. We are dealing not with fifteen million colored people, we are dealing with hundreds of millions. . . . However, I did say, in passing, that it was unthinkable to me that any people would take up arms in the name of an Eastland to go against anybody, and, gentlemen, I still say that. I thought it was healthy for Americans to consider whether or not Negroes should fight for people who kick them around.

"What should happen, would be that this U.S. Government should go down to Mississippi and protect my people. That is what should happen."

Chairman Walter, co-author of the racist Walter-McCarran Immigration Act which I shall describe in a later chapter, did not like what I was saying and he started banging his gavel for me to stop. But I wasn't quite finished and I went on to say:

> "I stand here struggling for the rights of my people to be full citizens in this country. They are not—in Mississippi. They are not—in Montgomery. That is why I am here today. . . . You want to shut up every colored person who wants to fight for the rights of his people!"

Following that hearing, I was deeply moved and gratified by many comments in the Negro press which showed a sympathetic understanding of the position I took in Washington. Since not a line about Negro editorial opinion on this subject appeared in the white newspapers of this country, which never miss a chance to scandalize my name and to quote any Negro who can be induced to do so, let me here give excerpts from some of the Negro newspaper comments on my testimony:

Afro-American (Baltimore), June 23, 1956:

"MR. ROBESON IS RIGHT

"If he stands up before a Congressional committee and tells its members what colored people are saying all over the nation with reference to segregation, disfranchisement and discrimination on account of color, he's only doing in Washington what's being done in the rest of the U.S. by red-blooded Americans, white and colored. . . .

"We agree with Mr. Robeson that its [the Commit-

tee's] members could more profitably spend their time
. . . bringing in for questioning such un-American elements as those white supremacists and manifesto signers
who have pledged themselves to defy and evade the very
Constitution they had previously sworn to uphold and
maintain."

Sun-Reporter (San Francisco), June 23, 1956:

"Robeson as far as most Negroes are concerned occupies
a unique position in the U.S., or the world, for that matter. Whites hate and fear him simply because he is the
conscience of the U.S. in the field of color relations.
Those Negroes who earn their living by the sweat of
their brows and a few intellectuals idolize the man. He
says the things which all of them wish to say about color
relations, and the manner in which he says these things
attracts the eye of the press of the world."

Charlottesville-Albemarle Tribune (Virginia), June 22,
1956:

"THE HOUSE UN-AMERICAN ACTIVITIES COMMITTEE FIASCO

"Paul Robeson is a great artist and a deeply sympathetic
human being. His own success did not blind him to the
wrongs suffered by his race. . . . To deny him the right to
travel, to sing and to speak as he pleases; to put him in
the pillory of a Congressional Committee and let lesser
men bait him, is more hurtful to American prestige abroad
than any intemperate statement he ever made."

Pittsburgh Courier (Pennsylvania), July 7, 1956:

"There is a great fear that he would embarrass the U.S.
abroad in regard to the Negro question. This is sheer
foolishness. The world is well aware of the treatment
which America accords its Negro population. The foreign
press on occasion gives more space to these events than
the American press. . . . The Till case, the Autherine
Lucy case and other such events are world property.
What on earth could Robeson say that has not already
been said about these sad affairs? . . . This denial is
robbing him of some of the most important years of his
life."

California Voice (Oakland), June 22, 1956:

"Robeson embodies the unrestrained and righteous rage that has broken bonds. His is the furious spirit wearied with tedious checker playing that stretches through nearly a hundred years in order to gain the rights guaranteed a hundred years ago.

"Robeson's cry is for justice, happiness and freedom here and now, while we live, not in some far away time in the future. His is the voice . . . that shouts down the promises of by-and-by and bellows 'No! Now!'

"A sensitive, tormented soul, he is that Other Self, the Alter Ego that a million Negroes try in self defense to disown. His protest is the authenic Protest of the Negro. . . . And when Paul Robeson says, 'I don't think a Negro will fight for an Eastland,' Robeson is right."

None of these newspapers is left-wing in character, and, in making their comments from which I have quoted, several of them made that fact perfectly clear. "We are not Communists," said the *Afro-American,* "nor do we follow the Communist line. Moreover, we do not approve of some of the activities and statements attributed to Mr. Robeson."

That's fair enough, I say, and while expressing my heartfelt gratitude for the understanding shown by the Negro press for my basic position, let me also say this: How much more *democratic* are my people's newspapers than are the general newspapers of our country! Here is an example of a quality of spirit that the Negro people have in abundance and which is so lacking in much of American life. The crusade for freedom that they are interested in is right here at home. Americans who wish for peace among nations—and I believe the vast majority of them do—can join with my people in singing our old-time song—

> *I'm going to lay down my sword and shield*
> *Down by the riverside . . .*
> *I'm going to study war no more!*

At Paris in 1949, I was convinced—and time has only served to deepen that conviction—that a war with the Soviet Union, a Third World War, was unthinkable for *anybody* who is not out of his mind. Certainly the majority of the colored peoples of the world have since made it clear that they want peace, and at their great conference held in Bandung, Indonesia, in 1955 they united on a program to promote peace. The reason why war is unthinkable to the peoples of Asia and Africa is spelled out in these words from the resolution adopted at Bandung:

> "The Conference considered that disarmament and the prohibition of the production, experimentation and use of nuclear and thermonuclear weapons of war are imperative to save mankind and civilization from the fear and prospect of wholesale destruction. It considered that the nations of Asia and Africa assembled here have a duty towards humanity and civilization to proclaim their support for disarmament and for prohibition of these weapons and to appeal to nations principally concerned and to world opinion, to bring about such disarmament and prohibition."

I would have liked to have gone to that historic gathering as an observer, but since my passport was denied I sent a message of greetings. (That message was itself later cited by the State Department as still another reason why I should not be permitted to travel!) In my message to Bandung, as in my speech at Paris, I stressed the urgent necessity of preventing another war and pointed out the direct interest that the colored peoples have in the maintenance of peace. I wrote:

> "Discussion and mutual respect are the first ingredients for the development of peace among nations. If other nations of the world follow the example set by the Asian-African nations, there can be developed an alternative to the policy of force and an end to the threat of H-Bomb war. The people of Asia and Africa have a direct interest in such a development since it is a well known fact that atomic weapons have been used only against the peoples of Asia. There is at present a threat to use them once more against an Asian people.
> "I fully endorse the objectives of the Conference to

prevent any such catastrophe, which would inevitably
bring about suffering and annihilation to all the peoples
of the world. Throughout the world all decent people
must applaud the aims of the Conference to make the
maximum contribution of the Asian and African countries
to the cause of world peace."

I also pointed out that the meeting of colored peoples of
the East was highly significant to colored peoples of the West
as well:

"To the Negro people of the United States and the
Caribbean Islands it was good news—great good news—to
hear that the Bandung Conference had been called 'to
consider problems of special interest . . . racialism and
colonialism.' Typical of the Negro people's sentiments are
these words from one of our leading weekly newspapers
[New York *Amsterdam News*]: 'Negro Americans should
be interested in the proceedings at Bandung. We have
fought this kind of fight for more than 300 years and have
a vested interest in the outcome.'"

No one can doubt that we do indeed have that "vested interest," and we ought to reach out in every way possible to
strengthen our ties with the rising world's majority. As for
me, when anyone asks me today what is the viewpoint I support in world affairs, I point to the Ten Principles of Bandung
which are as follows:

1. Respect for fundamental human rights and for the
   purposes and principles of the Charter of the United
   Nations.
2. Respect for the sovereignty and territorial integrity
   of all nations.
3. Recognition of the equality of all races and of the
   equality of all nations large and small.
4. Abstention from intervention or interference in the
   internal affairs of another country.
5. Respect for the right of each nation to defend itself
   singly or collectively, in conformity with the Charter
   of the United Nations.
6. (a) Abstention from the use of arrangements of collective defense to serve the particular interests of any
   of the big powers.

(b) Abstention by any country from exerting pressures on other countries.

7. Refraining from acts or threats of aggression or the use of force against the territorial integrity or political independence of any country.

8. Settlement of all international disputes by peaceful means, such as negotiations, conciliation, arbitration or judicial settlement as well as other peaceful means of the parties' own choice, in conformity with the Charter of the United Nations.

9. Promotion of mutual interests and cooperation.

10. Respect for justice and international obligations.

These principles I wholeheartedly support. On this platform I take my stand.

Chapter 2

"LOVE WILL FIND OUT THE WAY"

MY EXPERIENCES ABROAD, in the twelve years (1927-1939) that I made my home in London, brought me to understand that, no matter where else I might travel, my home-ground must be America. That point came up during the Congressional committee hearing when, after I had said that "in Russia I felt for the first time like a full human being—no color prejudice like in Mississippi, no color prejudice like in Washington," one of the committee members angrily demanded: "Why did you not stay in Russia?"

"Because my father was a slave," I retorted, "and my people died to build this country, and I am going to stay right here and have a part of it, just like you. And no fascist-minded people will drive me from it. Is that clear?"

Well, let me here try to make it clear how I came to feel that way. It was in Britain—among the English, Scottish, Welsh and Irish people of that land—that I learned that the essential character of a nation is determined not by the upper classes, but by the common people, and that the common people of all nations are truly brothers in the great family of mankind. If in Britain there were those who lived by plundering the colonial peoples, there were also the many millions who earned their bread by honest toil. And even as I grew to feel more Negro in spirit, or African as I put it then, I also came to feel a sense of oneness with the white working people whom I came to know and love.

This belief in the oneness of humankind, about which I have often spoken in concerts and elsewhere, has existed within me side by side with my deep attachment to the cause of my own race. Some people have seen a contradiction in this duality: white people who have seen me as a "citizen of the world," singing the songs of many lands in the languages of those peoples, have wondered sometimes how I could be so partisan for the colored people; and Negroes, on the other hand, have wondered why I have often expressed a warm affection for peoples who seem remote and foreign to them. I do not think, however, that my sentiments are contradictory; and in England I learned that there truly is a kinship among us all, a basis for mutual respect and brotherly love.

My first glimpse of this concept came through song, and that is not strange, for the songs that have lived through the years have always been the purest expressions of the heart of humanity. Early in my professional musical career I had the great good fortune to become associated with Lawrence Brown, an extraordinarily gifted Negro composer and arranger, and over the years this association grew into a successful partnership and personal friendship. It was this musician who clarified my instinctive feeling that the simple, beautiful songs of my childhood, heard every Sunday in church and every day at home and in the community—the great poetic song-sermons of the Negro preacher and the congregation, the work songs and blues of my father's folk from the plantations of North Carolina—should become important concert material. Lawrence Brown, who also knew and played the folk music of other peoples, as well as the great classics of Western song literature (many of which are based on folk themes), was firm in his conviction that our music—Negro music of African and American derivation—was in the tradition of the world's great folk music.* And so for my first five years as a singer my repertoire consisted entirely of my people's songs.

Then I went on to learn the songs of other peoples, and in

----

* See Appendix C, page 115, for a technical discussion of this subject.

Britain there was at hand the riches of English, Welsh and Gaelic folk-songs. And as I sang these lovely melodies I felt that they, too, were close to my heart and expressed the same soulful quality that I knew in Negro music. Others had noted this kinship before me, and in his autobiography Frederick Douglass, recalling the songs "both merry and sad" that he had heard as a plantation slave, wrote: "Child as I was, these wild songs depressed my spirit. Nowhere outside of dear old Ireland, in the days of want and famine, have I heard sounds so mournful." (Douglass had visited Ireland in 1847.) And in Scotland, Marjory Kennedy-Fraser, a noted contemporary authority on Gaelic folk-song, has suggested that Negro song is a direct product of her own people's culture. Without going into a discussion here of that claim, it is interesting to note Miss Kennedy-Fraser's viewpoint, expressed in the foreword to one of her collections, *Songs of the Hebrides*:

> "As I write, I am on a short visit to the American Middle West, and Dvorak's use of Negro melodies in his New World Symphony comes to mind. The Celts, alike of Scotland and Ireland, claim no inconsiderable share in the best of so-called Negro melodies of America, Hebridean younger sons, among others, becoming planters in the South two centuries ago, and taking with them Gaelic nurses with Celtic croons. And the Negroes learnt not only the croons but also the Gaelic tongue. And a woman of the Isles arriving in the South, it is told, had the fear on her that day, for did she not think that the blackness of the Gaelic-speaking Negro was the blackness of the sun on one of her own folk!"

Nevertheless, as we know, an appreciation of another people's art cannot by itself bridge the gulf which separates one people from another. Lovers of African sculpture can be quite indifferent to the people whose hands have wrought those masterpieces, and here in America there have been many who have appreciated—and appropriated—Negro music while showing an utter disregard for its creators. In my case, the tender beauty of their folk-songs drew me spiritually close to the common peoples of Europe; but it was the ominous drumbeat of current history that brought me to stand physically among them.

The years that I lived abroad witnessed the rise of fascism: the crash of martial music and the sound of marching jackboots drowned out the songs of peace and brotherhood. In 1933 Hitler rose to power in Germany and the raucous voice of the "Master Race" heralded the coming horror. In Italy a self-styled Caesar, who wore not toga but blackshirt, set out to win an empire; and in 1935 Mussolini's fascist legions marched against Ethiopia, and bomber and tank triumphed over musket and spear. At Geneva the League of Nations was deaf to Haile Selassie's desperate plea for sanctions against the aggressor as they were deaf to Litvinov's warning that peace was indivisible.

Then, the next year, came Spain—the attack on the Spanish Republic by the fascist traitor Franco, backed by the armed might of Hitler and Mussolini. It was a dress rehearsal for World War II: the rubble of the Spanish village of Guernica, leveled by air bombardment, was the pattern of destruction that soon would come upon Rotterdam and Warsaw, Coventry and Stalingrad—and finally, to Berlin itself. The Western powers were calm and unmoving in the face of the agony of Ethiopia and Spain. The governments that had refused to vote sanctions against Fascist Italy imposed an embargo on arms for Republican Spain; and they were indifferent to the Nazi terror unleashed in Germany against Social Democrats and Communists, liberals and trade unionists, Jews and other so-called "inferior races."

In England, in the great country houses where I had often been welcomed as guest, having tea and exchanging smiles with Lord and Lady This-and-that, a quiet serenity prevailed. Hitler and Mussolini?—well, they might very well be "bounders," uncouth fellows really and quite unacceptable socially, but upper-class England was rather pleased by what the dictators were doing. After all, the Nazi-fascist partnership

was based on the "anti-Comintern Pact" and they were out
to save all the great houses of Europe from the menace of
"Bolshevism"; and in Germany and Italy there was no longer
any nonsense from Labor, and business went ahead much
better with no trade unions. As for war, well, that was all
nicely taken care of at the Munich Conference where Czecho-
slovakia was sacrificed to Hitler, and if the Nazis did march,
they would surely go eastward—and that wouldn't be bad
at all, would it?

But in Britain the umbrella of appeasement that was held
high by Chamberlain did not obscure the portents seen in
the skies by the common people, and everywhere they rallied
for anti-fascist action. The heart of this movement was the
forces of Labor—the trade unions, the cooperatives, the political parties of the Left—but other broad sections of the
population were involved, including many from the middle
class and people from the arts, sciences and professions. And
so it was that I, as an artist, was drawn into that movement
and I came to see that the struggle against fascism must take
first place over every other interest.

In a radio broadcast that I made from the Continent to a
great London rally in defense of Spain, I explained my stand:

> "Every artist, every scientist, must decide *now* where
> he stands. He has no alternative. There is no standing
> above the conflict on Olympian heights. There are no
> impartial observers. Through the destruction, in certain
> countries, of the greatest of man's literary heritage,
> through the propagation of false ideas of racial and na-
> tional superiority, the artist, the scientist, the writer is
> challenged. The struggle invades the formerly cloistered
> halls of our universities and other seats of learning. The
> battlefront is everywhere. There is no sheltered rear."

And I saw, too, that the struggle for Negro rights was an
inseparable part of the anti-fascist struggle and I said:

> "The artist must elect to fight for Freedom or for
> Slavery. I have made my choice. I had no alternative.

The history of this era is characterized by the degradation of my people—despoiled of their lands, their culture destroyed, denied equal protection of the law, and deprived of their rightful place in the respect of their fellows.

"Not through blind faith or coercion, but conscious of my course, I take my place with you. I stand with you in unalterable support of the lawful government of Spain, duly and regularly chosen by its sons and daughters."

I went to Spain in 1938, and that was a major turning point in my life. There I saw that it was the working men and women of Spain who were heroically giving "their last full measure of devotion" to the cause of democracy in that bloody conflict, and that it was the upper class—the landed gentry, the bankers and industrialists—who had unleashed the fascist beast against their own people. From the ranks of the workers of other lands volunteers had come to help in the epic defense of Madrid, and in Spain I sang with my whole heart and soul for these gallant fighters of the International Brigade. A new, warm feeling for my homeland grew within me as I met the men of the Abraham Lincoln Battalion— the thousands of brave young Americans who had crossed the sea to fight and die that another "government of the people, by the people and for the people shall not perish from the earth." My heart was filled with admiration and love for these white Americans, and there was a sense of great pride in my own people when I saw that there were Negroes, too, in the ranks of the Lincoln men in Spain. Some of them, like Oliver Laws and Milton Herndon, were to be among the heavy casualties suffered by the volunteers and would be buried with their white comrades in the Spanish earth . . . a long way from home. From home? Yes, from America, my own home, and I knew in my heart that I would surely return there some day.

Spain—the anti-fascist struggle and all that I learned in it— brought me back to America. For another year I remained in Britain, and the more I became part of the Labor movement the more I came to realize that my home should be in America. I recall how a friend in Manchester deepened my understanding of the oneness of mankind as he explained how closely together the two of us were bound by the web of history and human suffering and aspiration. He told me of the life of bitter hardship and toil which his father and grandfather had known in the mills of that great textile center in England, and of how the cotton which his forefathers wove linked them with other toilers whose sweat and toil produced that cotton in faraway America—the Negro slaves, my own people, my own father. The workers of Manchester had supported the side of Abolition in the American Civil War, though the Union blockade of the South cut off the supply of cotton and resulted in greater hardship for them, while at the same time the mill-owners and their government had supported the side of Slavery. So here was a further insight and understanding of those forces in world life which make for common interests and make real the concept of international brotherhood.

The miners of Wales, who gave great support to the antifascist movement, welcomed me when I came to sing in behalf of aid to Spain and invited me into their union halls and into their homes. The Welsh miners, and other workers whom I met throughout England and Scotland, made it clear that there was a closer bond between us than the general struggle to preserve democracy from its fascist foes. At the heart of that conflict, they pointed out, was a class division, and although I was famous and wealthy, the fact was I came from a working-class people like themselves and therefore, they said, my place was with them in the ranks of Labor.

Well, there were not just bosses in America, I reflected; there were workers, too. If I had found the hand of brotherhood here among these working people of Britain, I ought to be able to find that hand in America as well. Above all, I must be among the Negro people during the great world crisis that was looming, and be part of their struggles for the new world a-coming that they sought. I would bring them, I planned, a message about Africa and would try to build a unity between them and their struggling kinfolk in the colonies. As artist and citizen, as a Negro and a friend of Labor, there should be plenty for me to do at home. I returned in 1939. . . .

In these last seven years, during which I have been cut off from personal contact with my friends in other lands, I have often reflected on the truth expressed in the words of a song that I have sung at many a concert—"Love will find out the way." By mail, by telephone and telegram, and through friends who have visited abroad, I have received many warm messages of friendship and good cheer from people throughout the world. And through the written word, by recordings and filmed interviews I have tried to keep in touch with audiences abroad whose numerous invitations for concert, stage and film appearances I was not free to accept.

A great joy during the period when I was not even permitted to travel to Canada (for which no passport is required from the United States), were the concerts at the border that were sponsored by the metal miners of Canada. In 1952 I had been invited to attend the Canadian convention of their union, the Mine, Mill and Smelter Workers, and when the State Department barred me from coming to them, the miners arranged for a concert to be held at Peace Arch Park, on the border between the State of Washington and the Province of British Columbia. I shall always remember that concert on May 18, 1952, when 30,000 Canadians came from many miles away to hear me, to demonstrate their friendship and to protest against all barriers to cultural exchange.

For three more years these concerts were held at that border, until finally the State Department was forced to retreat from its arbitrary and illegal ban on my travel to places which require no passport. The hand of brotherhood—yes, I found that hand in Canada, too.

Only a few weeks ago—this autumn of 1957—I had the wonderful experience of singing once again for the miners of Wales. They had sponsored an Eisteddfod—a traditional cultural festival of the Welsh people—and arrangements were made for me to sing for them by telephone. I cannot say how deeply I was moved on this occasion, for here was an audience that had adopted me as kin and though they were unseen by me I never felt closer to them. A few days later I received a letter from the National Union of Mineworkers, South Wales area, which said:

> "The trans-Atlantic transmission was a huge success, not only from the standpoint of reception but more so, from the inspiring effect it had upon the five thousand or more people gathered at our Eisteddfod. If you could only have seen this great body of people clinging to every note and word, you would have known the extent of the feeling that exists in Wales for you and for your release from the bondage now forced upon you.
>
> W. Paynter, President."

The first of such concerts-by-telephone had been arranged earlier in the year, on May 26, when I sang to an audience of a thousand in London. That concert was held in connection with a conference sponsored by the National Paul Robeson Committee, a group of distinguished people in Britain whose statements and activities are quite unknown in our country. Indeed, we have yet to see a single line on that subject in the general "free press" of our land, including the New York *Times* which boasts that through its far-flung newsgathering facilities it gives its readers "all the news that's fit to print." So, presumably, the news that more than a score of Members of Parliament are sponsors of that committee, and that many other prominent persons—writers, scholars, actors, lawyers, trade union leaders, titled personages, etc.—are also associated with that movement, is deemed bad for Americans to read and so it has been completely suppressed.

During the past seven years many people in Britain have spoken as individuals and through their organizations for my right to visit them again—as numerous others have in many other lands—and in March of 1956 a national movement was launched at a conference in Manchester. In a speech on that occasion, Mr. R. W. Casasola, president of the Foundry Workers Union, said that

". . . we are assembled in 1956 to ask that a little book be given to a gentleman with his photo in it and the statement that he is an American by birth. Here where the Chartists met to map the first struggle for the free vote, we launch a struggle for the right of all human beings to leave their country at any time and return at any time. America must get back to the principles of the Mayflower pilgrims, who sailed from this country seeking freedom, before its name stinks all over the world."

I sent a message to that conference in which I tried to express that which no words could ever truly express—my heartfelt gratitude for all that the British people were doing in this case, and I said:

"It is deeply moving for me to know that you and so many others throughout Britain are speaking out in behalf of my right to travel, my right to resume my career as an international artist which I began some thirty years ago. Though I must send you these words from afar, I can say that never have I felt closer to you than I do today. The warmth of your friendship reaches out across the barriers which temporarily separate us and rekindles the memories of many happy years that I spent among you."

In this message I recalled the last time I had been in Manchester, when the people there rallied to support the rights of my people in America:

"And I remember so well my last visit to Manchester in 1949—the warmth of your welcome at the Arena—the thousands who assembled to support our struggle in America to save the lives of the 'Trenton Six.' That struggle, as you know, was won; the Negro youths who had been sentenced to die in the electric chair were freed. The people of Manchester and other British cities, and people of many lands, had a great share in that victory."

In the spring of 1957 I was overjoyed to hear that the British Actors' Equity Association, at their annual meeting in London, had passed a resolution in favor of my coming to England. Here are a few lines from the report on that action published in the London *Times*:

". . . Mr. Guy Verney moved a resolution that the Council support the efforts being made to enable Mr. Robeson to sing here. Neither the English theatre nor the world could afford to waste a talent like Mr. Robeson's for an 'irrelevant reason' . . . Mr. Verney said that so far as he knew there was no sinister international underground movement putting forward the resolution, which was a request by artists to be enabled to hear, and work with, a great international artist. . . . The composite resolution was carried."

On May 4, 1957, the *Manchester Guardian* printed the following report:

"A letter signed by 27 M.P.'s [Members of Parliament] states that the Cooperative Party and the British Actors' Equity Association have added their support to the campaign to invite Mr. Robeson to sing in Britain and to ask the U. S. Government to allow him to come. The letter states that because of his political views—'which we regard as wholly irrelevant to the issue of freedom of travel and of the arts, although we do not necessarily agree with any of them'—Mr. Robeson's Government saw fit to deny the right to hear him to millions of British people who wanted to do so. In effect, since he was 'blacklisted' in his own country, Mr. Robeson was barred from practicing his profession. The signatories believe that there was 'never a more vital time for free countries to uphold their professions with regard to freedom of travel, as solemnly undertaken in the U.N. Declaration of Human Rights.' The letter concludes: 'Is this not doubly important in the case of so outstanding an artist as Paul Robeson, who properly belongs to all humanity?'"

Recently I received a letter, dated October 16, 1957, from Mr. Glen Byam Shaw, C.B.E., Director of the Shakespeare Memorial Theatre, inviting me to take part in their 1958 season at Stratford-upon-Avon. Such an invitation is truly a great honor to anyone in the theatre anywhere, but will the State Department permit me to go? Certainly I shall make still another request for a passport, as I have done in response to the many invitations that have come from countries other than Britain—for concert appearances on the Continent and elsewhere, for a role in a Soviet film production, and other similar offers

In the next chapter I will deal with the issues in my passport case, but here I would like to relate another experience in my efforts to function somehow, despite all barriers, as an international artist.

Friends in Europe were working on an important cultural project—a film sponsored by the World Federation of Trade Unions—and they wanted me to record a song to be used in the production. That was the gist of a letter that came to me in the summer of 1954. The letter was brief and few details were given. The words and music of the song were enclosed, but lyricist and composer were unnamed. The lyrics were in German, but the song was to be sung in English. The various verses and choruses were to be sung in the precise number of seconds specified for each; and I was to sing unaccompanied (no doubt an orchestra would be put "under" my voice in the finished version).

It was a song for peace and freedom, a song of brotherhood for working people of all lands—of course I would do it.

But how? I remembered how it was in London and Hollywood when I sang for films . . . the elaborate, soundproof studios with perfect acoustics, the director, his assistant, the sound engineers, the conductor with his earphones, the orchestra in full array, the small army of technicians and propmen, the clutter of expensive equipment—and the only thing I had to do was sing! Evidently this would have to be a little different. Now I must be some sort of associate producer here in New York for a film being made somewhere in Europe. Well, all right. . . .

Producer Robeson's first task was not difficult: he instructed Singer Robeson to get busy learning the song. Time was short and the singer could practice it in German until the producer could find someone to write the English version. As I did not then have a house of my own, the "studio" for this production would be my brother's home in Harlem—the parsonage of the church where he is pastor. And soon there could be heard in his study the new song that I was practicing:

"*Old Man Mississippi wütet,*
Schleppt uns unser Vieh weg und das Land sogar . . ."

It was a stirring song of six mighty rivers—the Mississippi, the Ganges, the Nile, the Yangtse, the Volga, the Amazon—and of the people who toil in their fertile valleys; and there was beauty and passion in the German lyrics. But English lyrics were required, and one day when a friend, the writer Lloyd Brown, stopped by during one of the rehearsals, I told him about the project. Would he like to help out by putting the words into English? He agreed, and soon there was a new version to be practiced:

"*Old Man Mississippi rages,*
Robs us of our cattle, plunders field and shore . . ."

Fine . . . the singer was ready now with words and music, but what about making the recording, Mr. Producer? Time is short, you said.

Here was another problem. The large recording companies belong to Big Business and would flatly refuse to rent their studios for such a job; and the smaller companies would be afraid. Then, too, there were recent experiences of sabotage done by recording engineers whose ears, keenly attuned to the snarls of McCarthy, were deaf to a singer of Peace.

My son had the answer. Paul, Jr, is an electrical engineer, and in recent years has become quite expert in making recordings. He would be the sound engineer for this job; and his portable equipment would be set up in the parsonage for the recording session.

Conditions were not exactly ideal when we came to make the recording. The small children in the household could be admonished to be silent (*Sh! Uncle Paul is trying to make a record!*), and the telephone disconnected lest it ring, but who could guarantee that a taxi would not honk on the busy street outside and spoil a perfect "take"? Under the circumstances it would have been forgivable had the producer shown signs of being disconcerted, but in this case he was too busy playing the part of singer and keeping an eye on his son who stood across the room, frowning with fierce concentration at a stop watch in one hand, the other poised overhead to signal the split second when each verse must end.

Well, taxis did honk, and a small boy shouted, and an airliner roared over the roof, and the six rivers of the song became sixty through all the re-takes—but finally the job was done. The mighty rivers now ran their courses on a thin ribbon of magnetic tape that was packed into a little box and sent across the sea. . . .

Months later we were delighted to read clippings from the European press which told of a new documentary film titled "Song of the Rivers," made by the great Dutch moviemaker, Joris Ivens. It was, said the critics, "a masterpiece," "a monumental work," "a hymn to Man, honoring labor and assailing colonialism." The reviewers described as "magnificent" the score, composed for the film by . . . Shostakovich! And the "unknown" lyricist was the famous German writer, Bertolt Brecht. The commentary was written by Vladimir Pozner, the noted French novelist; and Picasso was making a poster to publicize the film!

Masters of culture, champions of peace—what a wonderful film-making company I had become associated with! And there was a warm glow of appreciation for the invitation they had sent me, making it possible for a Negro American to join with Hollander and Russian and German and Frenchman and all the others in creative work for peace and liberation.

A year later, when I had the chance to visit Canada, I was very happy to see, in a trade union hall, this film which had carried the song from a house in Harlem to audiences around the world. Millions in many lands have seen "Song of the Rivers," and heard the commentary in Arabic, Japanese, Persian, Chinese, Czech, Slovak, Polish, English, Russian, French and many other languages; but people in the United States have been denied that opportunity.

But we know that such films for peace shall one day be welcomed to our land again, and singers of peace shall be given passports to travel abroad. No barriers can stand against the mightiest river of all—the people's will for peace and freedom now surging in floodtide throughout the world!

Chapter 3

OUR RIGHT TO TRAVEL

MY PASSPORT CASE is but one of several that have been brought into the Federal courts in recent years, challenging the power of the Passport Office of the State Department to decide that one or another applicant shall not be permitted to travel abroad. Whenever the Washington office-holders have decided in their own minds that such travel is "contrary to the best interests of the United States," passports have been denied. The Constitutional issues that are involved in these court cases, including my own, may soon be ruled upon by the Supreme Court; but it is not my intention here to discuss the legalistic aspects of this question. Nor is it my intention here to discuss the matter from the viewpoint of the personal wrongs I have suffered by being denied a passport. Suffice it to say that, while no one has charged that I have broken any law, I have been forced to suffer the loss of many thousands of dollars in fees offered to me as an artist in contracts that I have been unable to accept; and the legal expense of fighting my case for the past seven years has been considerable.

What concerns me here is the question of the right to travel in relation to the subject of Negro rights. The State Department will tell you that the fact that I am an advocate of Negro rights has nothing to do with the case, and to some people this might seem to be true since white persons as well as Negroes have been denied passports in this "cold-war" period. Nevertheless, there are facts—indisputable facts— which indicate that my concern for Negro rights is indeed at the heart of the case in which I am involved.

When my passport was revoked in 1950 (I had held one since 1922), I took the matter to court; and from the outset it was apparent that the Negro question was the crux of the matter. The State Department's brief, submitted to the Court of Appeals hearing in February, 1952, contained the following revealing statement in opposition to my claim of the right to travel:

". . . Furthermore, even if the complaint had alleged, which it does not, that the passport was cancelled solely because of the applicant's recognized status as spokesman for large sections of Negro Americans, we submit that this would not amount to an abuse of discretion in view of appellant's frank admission that he has been for years extremely active politically in behalf of independence of the colonial people of Africa."

This attitude of the State Department should outrage every decent American, because the tradition of our country (which was itself born in a great revolution of colonies against alien rule) has always favored the concept that just government can exist only with the consent of the governed. For Negroes, the State Department's viewpoint must have even greater significance. When I, as a Negro American, can be restricted and charged with having acted against the "best interests of the United States" by working in behalf of African liberation, some very important questions arise: What are the best interests of *Negro* Americans in this matter? Can we oppose White Supremacy in South Carolina and not oppose that same vicious system in South Africa?

Yes, I have been active for African freedom for many years and I will never cease that activity no matter what the State Department or anybody else thinks about it. This is my right— as a Negro, as an American, as a man!

Not only do I deny that this activity makes me "un-American" but I say this: *Those who oppose independence for the colonial peoples of Africa are the real un-Americans!* No matter what any Washington officials may "decide," the verdict of history, which we are reading in the stormy events of our day, is unmistakably clear: Those forces which stand against the freedom of nations are not only wrong—they are doomed to utter defeat and dishonor! Our country is strong and mighty among the nations of the world, but America cannot survive if she insists upon bearing the burden of the crumbling system of Imperialism. The colonial peoples—the colored peoples of the world—are going to be free and equal no matter whose "best interests" are in the way.

But it simply is not true that the real interests of our country are opposed to colonial independence, and most Americans, white and Negro, are aware of that truth. Indeed, the fact that the men who direct our government feel it necessary to present their support of Imperialism in terms of defending the "Free World" is proof that the American people generally have a democratic outlook and believe in the independence of nations.

There are a great many Americans who are convinced that our Secretary of State, Mr. John Foster Dulles, has himself made many statements and has done many things which are contrary to the best interests of the United States (not to mention the virtually unanimous opinion held by the rest of the world on that subject). How, then, can such a man—who has been fittingly called "America's misguided missile" and whose "brink-of-war" policies have appalled mankind—arrogate to himself the power to pass judgment on another citizen and decide whether that person's travel is or is not in the "best interests of the United States"? As far as Negroes in particular are concerned, there is no white American, good or bad, high or low, who can arbitrarily rule on what is or is not in the best interests of the Negro people!

In presenting the State Department's position to a later Federal court hearing in my passport case, in 1955, U.S. Attorney Leo A. Rover said that Paul Robeson "during his concert tours abroad had repeatedly criticized the conditions of Negroes in the United States." I say: So what? I have criticized those conditions abroad as I have at home, and I shall continue to do so until those conditions are changed. What is the Negro traveler supposed to do—keep silent or lie about what is happening to his people back home? Not I! Furthermore, as long as other Americans are not required to be silent or false in reference to their interests, I shall insist that to impose such restrictions on Negroes is unjust, discriminatory and intolerable.

Our government may properly instruct its employees as to what they may or may not say when traveling abroad, but people who go abroad as private citizens are not servants of the State Department: on the contrary, the State Department is supposed to be the servant of the people. Hence, no job-holder in Washington has the legal or moral right to demand that any American traveler advocate the viewpoint of that official in order to get a passport. Patriotism—love of one's country and devotion to its people's interests—cannot be equated with the outlook of some Wall Street corporation lawyer who is appointed Secretary of State or with the views of some political office-seeker who is rewarded with the job of issuing passports. He who upholds the democratic principles of the Declaration of Independence and the Bill of Rights is no less a patriot when he does so abroad, and if such conduct is "embarrassing" to anyone at home—well, shame on him!

But apart from the general principles involved in this question, the fact is that speaking the truth abroad has been of great value to the struggle for Negro rights in America. It has always been in our *best* interests. However, before going into that matter, I should first say a word about the right to travel in connection with our people's struggle for freedom.

From the very beginning of Negro history in our land, Negroes have asserted their right to freedom of movement. Tens of thousands of Negro slaves, like my own father, traveled the Underground Railroad to freedom in the North—not only to the northern part of the United States but farther into

Canada. Many of these freedom-seekers were concerned with their people who were left behind in bondage, and they joined with good white Americans, their fellow-Abolitionists, in promoting such travel. From the days of chattel slavery until today, the concept of *travel* has been inseparably linked in the minds of our people with the concept of *freedom*. Hence, the symbol of a railroad train recurs frequently in our folklore—in spirituals and gospel songs, in blues and ballads—and the train is usually "bound for glory" and "heading for the Promised Land." And there are boats, too, like the "Old Ship of Zion" and the "Old Ark" that will take us over the waters to freedom and salvation.

Some of the runaway slaves went to foreign countries not to secure their own freedom but to gain liberation for their kinsmen in chains. The good work they did abroad lives on in our own time, for that pressure which comes today from Europe in our behalf is in part a precious heritage from those early Negro sojourners for freedom who crossed the sea to champion the rights of black men in America. There were free Negroes, too, who went abroad to speak the truth and to enlist support for their cause. One of these was Rev. Nathaniel Paul, pastor of the African Baptist Society in Albany, N. Y., who was sent to England by a group of Negro refugees in Canada to promote anti-slavery activity and to collect funds in their behalf. In 1833 he reported to the Abolitionist press at home what he was doing over there:

"I have been engaged, for several months past, in travelling through the country and delivering lectures upon the system of slavery as it exists in the United States, the condition of the free people of color in that country, and the importance of promoting the cause of education and religion generally among the colored people. My lectures have been numerously attended by from two to three thousand people, the Halls and Chapels have been overflown, and hundreds have not been able to obtain admittance. I have not failed to give Uncle Sam due credit for his 2,000,000 slaves; nor to expose the cruel prejudices

of the Americans to our colored race . . . to the astonishment of the people here. And is this, they say, republican
liberty? God deliver us from it."*

In those years, the struggle for the right of Negroes to attend schools was centered in the North where most of the
free Negroes lived, and while Rev. Paul was in England one
of the "Autherine Lucy" cases of that time occurred in Con-
necticut, where a Quaker woman, Prudence Crandall, was
jailed because she admitted Negro girls to a school that she
conducted. Rev. Paul wrote to the magistrate who had sentenced Miss Crandall and said that he was going to use the
case as an "excellent opportunity" to expose the oppression
of Negroes in the United States. And he went on to say:

> "Yes, sir, Britons shall know that there are men in
> America, and whole towns of them, too, who are not so
> destitute of true heroism but that they can assail a help-
> less woman, surround her house by night, break her
> windows, and drag her to prison, for the treasonable act
> of teaching females of color to read!!!"

William Wells Brown, another Negro agitator for freedom,
wrote to Wendell Phillips from London, in 1849:

> "So you see, my friend, that though we are denied
> citizenship in America and refused passports at home
> when wishing to visit foreign countries, they dare not re-
> fuse us a passport when we apply for it in Old England.
> There is a public sentiment here, that, hard-hearted as
> the Americans are, they fear. When will Americans learn,
> that if they would encourage liberty in other countries,
> they must practice it at home?"

That question today, a century later, rolls around the world
like thunder: *When will Americans learn, that if they would
encourage liberty in other countries, they must practice it at
home?* And let all honest people who have been misled by
the advocates of "Gradualism" reflect on the fact that a

---

* Herbert Aptheker, ed., *A Documentary History of the Negro People in the United States* (Citadel Press, New York, 1951), p. 139.
Several other historical references in this chapter are from that work.

hundred years have not softened the "hard-hearted" Negro-haters we still have in our land! Another comment is in order at this point. Although Negroes were denied passports to travel abroad in those days, passports were not required by law for such travel, and so it was possible for them to take their case before the court of world opinion and not be stopped by bigoted officials here who disapproved of their activity. Evidently, in this respect, our country is much less democratic in 1957 than it was in 1847.

Nevertheless, Negroes who spoke the truth abroad in the years of the Abolitionist struggle were bitterly denounced by the Big White Folks back home, and the U.S. newspapers called Frederick Douglass a "glib-tongued scoundrel" and said he was "running out against the institutions and people of America" when he traveled around Europe arousing anti-slavery sentiment. Defiantly, Douglass retorted:

> "I deny the charge that I am saying a word against the institutions of America, or the people as such. What I have to say is against slavery and the slaveholders. I want the slaveholder to feel he has no sympathy in England, Scotland or Ireland; that he has none in Canada, none in Mexico, none among the poor wild Indians; that the voice of the civilized, aye, and the savage world is against him. [Brother Douglass really wanted to reach *everybody!*] I would have condemnation blaze down upon him in every direction, till, stunned and overwhelmed with shame and confusion, he is compelled to let go the grasp he holds upon the persons of his victims and restores them to their long-lost rights."

Douglass, a runaway slave, the greatest of these Negro Abolitionist leaders, was offered a home, land, and the means for a good life for himself and his family in England; but he gratefully declined. In his famous farewell speech to the British people, he told why he was going back to America:

> "I do not go back to America to sit still, remain quiet, and enjoy ease and comfort. . . . I glory in the conflict, that I may thereafter exult in the victory. I know that

victory is certain. I go, turning my back upon the ease, comfort and respectability which I might maintain even here. . . . Still I will go back for the sake of my brethren. I go to suffer with them; to toil with them; to endure insult with them; to undergo outrage with them; to lift up my voice in their behalf; to speak and write in their vindication; and struggle in their ranks for the emancipation which shall yet be achieved."

This militant spirit of Douglass lives on today in the spirit of my people, but since his time we have seen that some Negro leaders have thought it advisable to travel abroad with tidings that all is well with their folks back home. One of the first of these Negro apostles of the "American way of life" was Booker T. Washington who tried to serve both the needs of his people and the interests of their oppressors. But in 1910, when Mr. Washington went to England to praise the treatment of his people in America, a distinguished group of Negro educators, doctors, lawyers, clergymen and editors signed an open message to the people of Europe which nailed his distortions and told the bitter truth of continuing Negro oppression at home.

"Against this dominant tendency [they wrote] strong and brave Americans, White and Black, are fighting, but they need, and need sadly, the moral support of England and Europe in their crusade for the recognition of manhood. . . . It is a blow in the face to have one, who himself suffers daily insult and humiliation in America, give the impression that all is well."

W. E. B. Du Bois, William Monroe Trotter, Bishop Alexander Walters, J. Max Barber and Archibald Grimké were among the signers of this historic document and so, too, was my Uncle Francis—N. F. Mossell, M.D., medical director of Douglass Hospital in Philadelphia. Always a staunch and encouraging friend to me, the late Dr. Mossell was the husband of my mother's sister, Gertrude.

To the Negro artist, as well as to the Negro spokesman, the "moral support of England and Europe" has been of great importance and, indeed, the right to travel has been a virtual necessity for the Negro artist. A century ago it was not possible for a Negro actor to appear on the American stage in any role—not even as a buffoon. (Such parts were reserved for "whites only" in the days of the black-face minstrel shows, and only toward the end of that era was "progress" made to the point where a Negro face was permitted to appear in the traditional burnt cork of that happily now-dead form of American theatre.) Hence, there was no place on our stages for one of the greatest actors in theatrical history—Ira Aldridge, a Negro. Still generally unknown to Americans is the enormous stature he gained in England and elsewhere in Europe as one of the most distinguished Shakespearean performers ever seen. Aldridge, who was born in New York around 1807, was the son of a Presbyterian minister, and was educated at the University of Glasgow. The door that was open to me in 1930 to play Othello in London was open to Aldridge in 1830 when he played the part at the Royalty Theatre of that city. Together with the noted Shakespearean artist Edmund Kean, who played Iago, Aldridge was enthusiastically acclaimed throughout the Continent as well—in France, Prussia, Sweden, Russia and Poland. He died in the latter country in 1867.

There is no need for me to list the many other Negro actors, singers and dancers who won a place in the arts through exercising their right to travel—their names would be practically a roster of Negro achievement in this field. Some of these artists decided, as was their right, to remain abroad—Josephine Baker in France, Wayland Rudd in the Soviet Union, Turner Layton in England, to mention only a few.

It must be clear to any fair-minded American that, in all our nation's history and today as well, the right to travel is of special importance to the Negro artist. In view of this fact, is it not unjust to require that he remain silent about the conditions of his people in order for him to have this opportunity to practice his art and to earn his livelihood?

In the heartfelt outburst that the events in Little Rock evoked from him, Louis Armstrong, the great musician who was scheduled to go to the Soviet Union, asked: "If the people over there ask me what is wrong with my country, what am I supposed to say?"

Well, I would reply: "Speak the truth that is in your heart, Brother Armstrong, the same as you would here on the streets of Harlem." And all of us Negroes should tell him: "If they victimize you for doing that, we will come to your defense. We will raise such a storm that no narrow-minded and prejudiced bureaucrat in Washington will dare to take away your passport!"

Indeed, isn't it a sin and a shame that we have not responded with vigorous protests against the denial of a passport to W. E. B. Du Bois? The stature and quality of Dr. Du Bois' life and work cannot be challenged: he is the foremost scholar and sage among us. He is the father of our freedom movement today. In wisdom of mind, integrity of character and selfless dedication to humanity our Dr. Du Bois is outstanding not only in Negro life: he is one of the truly great Americans of our century.

How monstrously evil it is, then, that the little men in high places have dared to say that such a man is not entitled to a passport, that he cannot travel abroad in a world which knows and honors him! Yet that is what has happened. Only a few years ago the unenlightened and unprincipled white men who rule this land brought Du Bois in manacles before a court of law and charged him with being a "foreign agent" because he dared to uphold the cause of world peace. That attempted frame-up was foiled and Du Bois was freed. But he is not free to travel.

Dr. Du Bois was invited to attend the celebration of the independence of Ghana, and the State Department barred his way, but of all the Americans who traveled to the Ghana celebration there was not one man by far who was as worthy of being there as was Du Bois. For over forty years he has championed the cause of African freedom, and his books were the first to reveal the truth about the relationship of Africa with the modern world. He was the founder and architect of the Pan-African movement, and under his pioneering leadership the first Pan-African Congress was assembled at Paris in 1919. Du Bois presided over the fifth Pan-African Congress in Manchester, England, in 1945, that was attended by Kwame Nkrumah, who later became the first prime minister of free Ghana, by Jomo Kenyatta and two hundred other leaders from every section of Africa, the West Indies, British Guiana, British Honduras, Brazil and the United States.

Truly, Dr. Du Bois' travels have been in the best interests not only of the people of the United States but in the best interests of the people of the world. How can we be silent, how can we rest until this great humanitarian, teacher and leader is given his right to travel?

To achieve the right of full citizenship which is our just demand, we must ever speak and act like free men. When we criticize the treatment of Negroes in America and tell our fellow citizens at home and the peoples abroad what is wrong with our country, each of us can say with Frederick Douglass:

"In doing this, I shall feel myself discharging the duty of a true patriot; for he is a lover of his country who rebukes and does not excuse its sins."

Chapter 4

THE TIME IS NOW

As I SEE IT, the challenge which today confronts the Negro people in the United States can be stated in two propositions:

1. Freedom can be ours, here and now: the long-sought goal of full citizenship under the Constitution is now within our reach.

2. We have the power to achieve that goal: what we ourselves do will be decisive.

These two ideas are strongly denied or seriously doubted by many in our land, and the denial and doubt are demonstrated both by action and inaction in the crisis of our time. Let me begin by discussing the first proposition.

Those who are openly our enemies—the avowed upholders of the myth of White Supremacy—have bluntly stated their position on the matter: Not now and not ever shall the Jim Crow system be abolished. *"Let me make this clear,"* declared Eastland, the foremost spokesman for this group, in a Senate speech ten days after the Supreme Court outlawed school segregation, *"the South will retain segregation."* And the strength of this viewpoint was shown when a hundred other Senators and Representatives from the South signed a manifesto in which they denounced the Court's decision and pledged that they would resist its enforcement. The whole world has seen how these defiant words have become defiant deeds.

Others, who claim to be our friends, insist that the immediate enforcement of our lawful rights is not possible. We must wait, we are told, until the hearts of those who persecute us have softened—until Jim Crow dies of old age. This idea is called "Gradualism." It is said to be a practical and constructive way to achieve the blessings of democracy for colored Americans. But the idea itself is but another form of race discrimination: in no other area of our society are lawbreakers granted an indefinite time to comply with the provisions of law. There is nothing in the 14th and 15th Amendments, the legal guarantees of our full citizenship rights, which says that the Constitution is to be enforced "gradually" where Negroes are concerned.

"Gradualism" is a mighty long road. It stretches back 100 long and weary years, and looking forward it has no end. Long before Emancipation was won, our people had learned that the promises of freedom in the future could not be trusted, and the folk-knowledge was put down in the bitter humor of this song from slavery days:

> *My old master promised me*
> *When he died he'd set me free,*
> *He lived so long that his head got bald*
> *And he gave up the notion of dying at all.*

Well, chattel slavery was finally abolished—not gradually but all at once. The slave-masters were never *converted* to liberal philosophy: they were *crushed* by the overwhelming force that was brought to bear against their rotten system. They were not asked to *give up,* penny by penny, the billions of dollars they owned in human property: the 13th Amendment *took* it all away in an instant.

Some of our "best friends" are really enemies, and "Gradualism" is but a mask for one of their double faces. But there are also well-intentioned white liberals and various Negro spokesmen, too, who honestly believe that the advancement of colored people can be made only gradually, that progress cannot be forced, that the reactionaries should not be pushed too hard, that five years or ten years, or even generations must pass before our civil wrongs can become civil rights.

And there are many of my people who, looking at a place like Mississippi, sadly shake their heads and say that it's going to be a long time before a real change comes about: the white bosses are too set in their ways and they are rotten mean to the bone.

The viewpoint that progress must be slow is rooted in the idea that democratic rights, as far as Negroes are concerned, are not inalienable and self-evident as they are for white Americans. Any improvement of our status as second-class citizens is seen as a matter of charity and tolerance. The Negro must rely upon the good will of those in places of power and hope that friendly persuasion can somehow and some day make blind prejudice see the light.

This view is dominant in the upper levels of government and society throughout the land. It is easy for the folks on the top to take a calm philosophical view and to tell those who bear the burden to restrain themselves and wait for justice to come. And, Lord knows, my people have been patient and long-suffering: they have a quality of human goodness, of tenderness and generosity that few others have. As the New York *Times* put it: "When one regards the violent history of nationalism and racism in the rest of the world, one must be thankful for the astonishing gentleness and good humor of the Negroes in the United States."

But patience can wear out—and if the patience of some of us wore out before that of others, it doesn't matter today. The plain fact is that a great many Negroes are thinking in terms of *now*, and I maintain and shall seek to prove that the goal of equal-rights-now can be achieved.

It has been said, and largely forgotten, that by the year 1963, the centennial of the Emancipation Proclamation, full freedom should be won. Well, I believe that still. The year of 1963 can indeed celebrate the winning of full citizenship rights, in fact and not only on paper, for every Negro in every city, county and state in this land. In 1963 a Negro statesman from Mississippi can be sitting in the Senate

seat now disgraced by Eastland, just as the Negro Senator
Hiram Revels once replaced the traitor Jeff Davis in that
same office. I say that Jim Crow—and "Gradualism" along
with it—can be buried so deep it can never rise again, and
that this can be done now, in our own time!

Is this but a dream, a fantasy that "can't happen here"?
For an answer let us look with our eyes wide open at the
world around us: let us look to the reality of our day, the
changed situation which indicates that the time is ripe, that
the opportunity is here.

The changed situation is this: *Developments at home and
abroad have made it imperative that democratic rights
be granted to the Negro people without further delay.* A
century has passed since Frederick Douglass pointed out
that "The relations subsisting between the white and black
people of this country is the central question of the age,"
and a half century since Dr. Du Bois proclaimed that "The
problem of the twentieth century is the problem of the Color
Line." Today we see that the prophetic truth of those
statements has grown a thousandfold, and that the time has
come when the question of the age and the problem of the
century must be resolved.

It is obvious today that the issue of Negro rights is a central question in our national life. A typical comment is that
of the editors of *Look* magazine who see in this issue
"America's greatest legal, political and emotional crisis since
the Civil War"; and typical, too, is the opinion of the New
York *Times* that "a social revolution with profound implications for domestic accord and world leadership confronts
this country today." But in all of the discussion of this question which fills the press and the air waves and which re-
sounds from platform, pulpit and conference table, little
light is shed on the basic factors that are involved.

It is not merely a matter of "domestic accord" that is
involved in our national crisis. The fact is that constitutional government in the United States cannot be main-

tained if Negroes are restricted to second-class citizenship. President Eisenhower, against his will and inclination, was compelled to recognize that the very structure of our government was imperiled by the defiance of Faubus in Little Rock; and for the first time since Reconstruction days Federal troops were moved in to uphold the Constitution. But the Administration and the dominant group it represents has not as yet been compelled to recognize an even more fundamental question: democracy cannot survive in a racist America. When a government spokesman appeals to the White Supremacists "to remember America as well as their prejudices," he reflects the persistent blindness of those who still hope to eat their cake and have it, too.

I say that it is utterly false to maintain, as so many do, that the crux of the issue is personal prejudice. In a baseball game, an umpire's decision may be based upon some prejudice *in his mind,* but a state law that makes it a crime for Negroes to play baseball with whites is a statute *on the books.* The Jim Crow laws and practices which deny equal rights to millions of Negroes in the South—and not only in the South!—are not private emotions and personal sentiments: they are a system of legal and extralegal *force* which violates and nullifies the Constitution of the United States.

We know that this condition has prevailed for many years, and it might be asked at this point: Why can't it go on like this for years to come? What compelling factor in our national life calls for a change at this time?

The answer is: The interests of the overwhelming majority of the American people demand that the Negro question be solved. It is not simply a matter of justice for a minority: what is at stake is a necessity for all. Just as in Lincoln's time the basic interests of the American majority made it necessary to strike down the system of Negro enslavement, so today those interests make it necessary to abolish the system of Negro second-class citizenship.

Increasingly it is becoming clear that the main roadblock

to social progress in our country—for labor, for education, for public health and welfare—is that very group which stubbornly opposes equal rights for Negroes. The 100 Congressional signers of the Southern manifesto against desegregation are not only the foes of the Negro minority: they are a powerful reactionary force against the people as a whole. Holding office by virtue of Negro disfranchisement and re-elected term after term by the votes of a handful of whites, these lawless Dixiecrats are lawmakers for the entire nation. The White Supremacy they espouse does not elevate the white workers in industry or the poor white farmers, and they have helped promote and maintain the economic process that has drained off most of the wealth from Southern resources and has made that section much poorer than the rest of the country.

The upholders of "states' rights" against the Negro's rights are at the same time supporters of the so-called "right-to-work" laws against the rights of the trade unions. The reactionary laws which have undermined the gains of Roosevelt's New Deal—the anti-labor Taft-Hartley Act, the anti-foreignborn Walter-McCarran Act, the thought-control Smith Act—all were strongly backed by the Dixiecrats in Congress. Until their political power is broken, there can be no real social or economic progress for the common people anywhere, North or South. Indeed, it is clear that not only will there be no progress, but there will be further retrogression unless this political cancer is removed from public life.

The attention of the nation is focused now on the words and deeds of those who are resisting the Supreme Court's decision that segregated schools are unlawful. The national conscience, which has for so long tolerated segregation as a "local custom," cannot and will not permit the defenders of Jim Crow to substitute mob violence and anarchy for constitutional government. The conflict today pertains mainly to the schools, but the signers of the Southern manifesto were not wrong when they saw the Court's decision as a threat to the "habits, customs, traditions and way of life" of White Supremacy. If the evil doctrine of "separate but equal" was struck down in reference to public schools, how can it be lawful in any other area of public life?

The die has been cast: segregation must go. The White Citizens Councils may foment mob resistance, and Southern senators and governors may rant and rave against a new Reconstruction, and the President may try to look the other way—but the vast majority of Americans, the indifferent and lukewarm as well as the most progressive, are not going to give up their democratic heritage in order to deny that heritage to fellow citizens who are colored.

We know, of course, that the democratic-minded majority is slow to move, and that the poison of race prejudice has deeply corroded the whole of our national life. The make-up of the Federal government is not too different from the state governments in the South: it, too, is a white man's government. Not a single Negro is a member of the powerful Senate and there are only three among the 435 members of the House of Representatives. Legislation in behalf of civil rights could not be defeated or emasculated by the Dixiecrats without the support of Congressmen from other parts of the country. In a later chapter more will be said about the situation of Negroes outside the South, but suffice it to say here that hypocrisy concerning Negro rights has existed throughout our land ever since the Declaration of Independence affirmed the truth that "all men are created equal." And so it must be recognized that if there were not another factor in addition to the domestic one, the changed situation I speak of might not exist.

That other factor—relentless, powerful, compelling—is the pressure of world opinion against racism in the United States. This pressure is widely recognized in our national life, and both the pressure and our recognition of it are constantly growing. The case of Emmett Till, lynched in Mississippi, and of Autherine Lucy, barred from the University of Alabama, aroused a storm of condemnation from beyond our borders; and the story of Little Rock—in words and pictures—shook the world. Indeed, the pressure of world opinion was itself an important factor in the very decision of the Supreme Court which evoked the defiance of the Arkansas governor. In his argument in support of school desegregation, the Attorney General of the United States reminded the high tribunal that "The existence of race discrimination against minority groups in the United States has an adverse effect upon our relations with other countries."

There is a lack of understanding in American life, however, as to the sources of this pressure which has been seen as a hostile force, endangering this country's rightful (and self-appointed) place of world leadership. The source of the pressure is said to be "Communist propaganda" among the colored peoples who comprise the majority of the world's population. Since the pressure arose from the dissemination of "lies" and "slander," it could be done away with by a "truth crusade" which would show that the situation of the American Negro was to be envied rather than deplored. Although it was evident to Negroes generally that the pressure could and did benefit the struggle for our rights (the speedy desegregation of schools, restaurants and hotels in Washington was an obvious case in point), a number of prominent Negroes offered their services in the grand campaign to take the pressure off! A rather unflattering comment about these individuals was recently made by a columnist in the New York *Amsterdam News:*

> "Our government has been employing Negro intellectuals, entertainers, ministers and many others to play the roles of ambassadorial Uncle Toms for years. They are supposed to show their well-fed, well-groomed faces behind the Iron Curtain as living proof that everyone is free and equal in the U.S., and the color bar is a myth."

Now, it is not my intention to engage in personal criticisms of any kind, and I know a number of performing

artists who went on these government-sponsored tours because they needed work and who were out to show the world,
as they did, that the American Negro has talent and dignity
deserving of respect anywhere. Yet it must be said that the
Negro spokesmen who have set out to calm the clamor of
world humanity against racism in America have done a
grievous disservice to both their people and their country.
To proclaim abroad that "A peaceful revolution has occurred
overnight; it is a mark of distinction to be a Negro in the
United States"—and those words were actually uttered by a
well-known Negro minister to an Asian audience—can do
nothing except to discredit the speaker.

By now it should be recognized by all that this global ad-
vertising campaign to deny the obvious has failed in its purpose. Facts still speak louder than words. The charge that
the foreign protests on this issue are provoked by "Communist propaganda" expresses contempt for the intelligence and
sensibilities not only of the colored peoples but of the democratic-minded people of all races and creeds. Of course, the
Communists of the world denounce racism: that's nothing
new and it seems rather silly to charge that this is some kind
of newfangled weapon of the "cold war" when anyone can
go to the library and read that Karl Marx said, a hundred
years ago, that "Labor in a white skin can never be free
while labor in a black skin is branded." But to assert that the
revulsion of world humanity against racist outrages in America is simply the result of Communist agitation can only
insult public opinion abroad, just as American public opinion
rejected as nonsense Eastland's charge that our Supreme
Court has been "indoctrinated and brainwashed by left-wing
pressure groups."

What, then, has brought about the persistent and growing
pressure from all parts of the world on this issue? One cause
is the shattering experience of World War II—the untold
havoc and horror committed by the Nazis in their drive to
win domination for their so-called Master Race. Millions were

slain and millions more suffered disaster. The world has learned the terrible lesson of Hitler: racism, backed by the power and technology of a modern industrial state, is a monster that must never be unleashed again. What difference is there between the Master Race idea of Hitler and the White Supremacy creed of Eastland? Who can convince the European peoples that the burning cross of the white-robed Klan is different from the swastika of the Brownshirts? America, of course, is not a fascist nation, but the deep-rooted racism here and its violent outbursts arouse the worst fears of those who survived the holocaust of Hitlerism.

Those who tell the world that racism in American life is merely a fading hangover from the past, and that it is largely limited to one section of our country, cannot explain away the infamous Walter-McCarran Immigration Act passed by Congress since the war. No decree of Nazi Germany was more foully racist than this American law which is, in the words of Senator Lehman, "based on the same discredited racial theories from which Adolf Hitler developed the infamous Nuremberg Laws." Look how our immigration quotas are allotted: from Ireland's 3 million people, 17,000 may come to our country each year; but from India, with her 400 millions, the quota is—100! Usually we Negroes do not think much about immigration laws because we've been here for centuries, but in our midst there are many from the West Indies, and their talents and vitality have been important to our communities far beyond their numbers. Under the Walter-McCarran law, with all of its provisions to reduce "non-Nordic" immigration, the number of Negroes who can come from the Caribbean or anywhere else has been drastically cut down.

After the defeat of Hitlerism, the nations came together in a worldwide organization; and our country, which had not belonged to the old League of Nations, became a leading force in the United Nations. Founded in San Francisco and making its headquarters in New York, the U.N. brought the eyes of the world upon the United States. From the outset,

Negro leaders of vision saw in the new organization a new opportunity to win backing for their people's democratic demands. Shortly before he was ousted from his leading post in the National Association for the Advancement of Colored People (which he had helped to found), Dr. Du Bois addressed an appeal for Negro rights to the U.N. In that historic document, he pointed out that racism in America was now an international problem. He wrote:

> "A discrimination practiced in the United States against her own citizens and to a large extent in contravention of her own laws, cannot be persisted in without infringing upon the rights of the peoples of the world. . . . This question, then, which is without doubt primarily an internal and national question, becomes inevitably an international question, and will in the future become more and more international as the nations draw together."

That is exactly what has come to pass, and those in our midst who were too blind to see that truth ten years ago can read it today in the headlines of the world. The U.N. itself reflects the great changes that have come about "as the nations draw together." Today there are twenty-nine nations in the Asian-African bloc in the U.N., and as the roll call of the General Assembly is taken we hear the names of new nations that are members now—among them African nations like Ghana and Sudan and others. Like a great barometer the U.N. registers the changing climate of the world as the wave of colonial liberation sweeps onward.

Here, then, in the changing bases of power abroad, is the main source of that pressure for changes at home. The era of White Supremacy, the imperialist domination of the East by a handful of Western nations, is rapidly coming to an end. A new era is being born. We, the Negro people of the United States, and of the Caribbean area as well, are a part of the rising colored peoples of the world. This is not merely a matter of racial identification and common sentiments: the course of history has made it so. The plunder of Africa by

the nations of Europe, which brought our ancestors to this
hemisphere as slaves, was the beginning of the era that
brought most of Asia, too, under white domination. Now
when that era is ending, it is inevitable that our own destiny
is involved.

Freedom is a hard-bought thing and millions are still in
chains, but they strain toward the new day drawing near.
In Kenya Colony, for example, the African patriots—the so-
called Mau Mau—are hunted like wild animals and the people's leader, Jomo Kenyatta, is jailed. I knew this brave man
well in the years that I lived in London; like Nehru of India
and many others from colonial lands who were my friends
in England, he dreamed of freedom for his people. Well,
Nehru was jailed in India, and many thousands more; but
the road to independence and power ran through those prison
walls, and Kenyatta, too, will travel on.

A new China has arisen, young in strength and ancient in
culture—a world power of half a billion people. This China
is a mighty big fact not to "recognize," yet there are some
stubborn statesmen in Washington who insist that "China"
consists of the island hideout where Chiang Kai-shek and
his outlaw gang are living off the American taxpayers' money.
But the real China's neighbors in Asia—the people of India,
Pakistan, Burma, Ceylon, Korea, Vietnam, Indonesia—recognize in her a powerful friend. So Prime Minister Nehru is
happy to shake hands with Chairman Mao, and Burma's pre-
mier, U Nu, has this to say about the leading power in the
Orient:

> "Although Burma has disliked communism at home, we
> are not meddling in the affairs of the Chinese who choose
> communism to suit their circumstances. Communist lead-
> ers in China have abolished foreign economic exploita-
> tion and wiped out bribery and corruption for the first
> time, thus winning the admiration of fellow Asians. They
> are building a new world for their masses."

(We Negroes should realize, when we read in the daily

newspapers denunciations of a newly emancipated country like China, that what we are told "ain't necessarily so." We might well remember that Douglass in his time, defending liberated Haiti from the newspaper charges that it was "a nation of cutthroats and robbers," observed that "white Americans find it hard to tell the truth about colored people. They see us with a dollar in their eyes.")

Washington may not yet recognize the new People's Republic of China that has arisen—and it certainly has changed a lot since the "good old days" when Europeans put up signs in the parks of Shanghai: "No Dogs or Chinese Allowed"— but the great conference of Asian and African free nations at Bandung welcomed new China to a place of leadership in their midst.

It is high time for Negro leadership to take a new look at the world beyond our borders and to stop parroting the fearful wails of Washington officialdom that Asia and Africa may be "lost to the Free World." No doubt there are some folks who stand to lose a great deal as the colonial peoples take over their own lands and resources, but what in the world do Negro Americans have to lose over there? *Our* problem is how to get some of that freedom and dignity that other colored folks are getting these days. What we have to be concerned about is what we can *get,* and not be worrying our heads about what the Big White Folks might *lose!*

Negro leadership would do well to ponder the significance of a recent event at the United Nations. On September 19, 1957, Mr. Dulles made a speech at the U.N. and although he said nothing new, repeating his stock charges that in Asia and Africa the Communists were "inciting nationalism to break all ties with the West," his words were reported throughout the country. The newspapers and radio ignored what the next speaker said, but I believe that his remarks had historical significance. The speaker was Ako Adjei, Minister of Justice of Ghana (on the west coast of Africa from whence so many of our ancestors came), and he told the General Assembly:

". . . Ghana has a special responsibility and obligation towards all African peoples or peoples of African descent throughout the world who are struggling to free themselves from foreign rule, *or even who, by the mere reason of their color, are denied the enjoyment of the very elementary civil and political rights which the Constitutions of their own states guarantee to all their citizens.* I should like to request all Members of the United Nations to take note that the new State of Ghana is concerned with the freedom of all African peoples and *also with the treatment that is meted out to all peoples of African descent, wherever they may be in any part of the world.* We appeal to the conscience of the nations, great or small, to join in the crusade for the observance of fundamental human rights and freedoms which are enshrined in the Charter of the United Nations." (Emphasis added.)

Amen, brother, amen! I am sure your message will be warm in the hearts of Africa's children all over this land.

Yes, the peoples of the free colored nations are our natural friends: their growing strength is also ours. When the Ambassador from India is Jim Crowed in Texas, and when the Finance Minister of Ghana is Jim Crowed in Delaware, they and their people feel exactly as we do. Diplomatic apologies are made to them, but they know that the President and the Secretary of State make no apology or restitution to the 16 millions of us who daily undergo the indignities of race discrimination, nor to the millions of others—the American Indians, the Mexican-Americans, the Puerto Ricans and people of Asian descent—who are insulted and outraged in this "Land of the Free." And so it is that the colored peoples, two-thirds of all mankind, are shouting that the Walls of Jericho must come tumbling down.

There are some diehard White Supremacists in our country who scorn the thought that public opinion abroad must be taken into account. Governor Timmerman of South Carolina told the press that "India isn't interested in the Negro— or the white man. It is ridiculous to think that these people worry about what Americans do." And he went on to advise that diplomats from colored nations should, when traveling in the South, stay "in the best available night hotels."

But fortunately for us—and even more fortunately for the country as a whole—the controlling group in national leadership is not that ignorant. Whatever may be their personal prejudices, the men who direct our foreign policy know beyond the shadow of a doubt that the United States cannot afford to ignore the pressure that comes from abroad. Race discrimination can cost us much more than national prestige: it can drastically hurt our national economy. Those who are vitally concerned with foreign trade and investment, with the raw materials our industries must get from other lands, are much more realistic and infinitely more powerful than ·are people like Eastland, Timmerman and Faubus. Faced with the fact that our country must co-exist, if it is to exist at all, with the new nations that have emerged, there can be no doubt that the powers-that-be in America will have to reckon with the new situation.

The viewpoint that I have presented above is not a hasty appraisal of the headline news and current events: it is based upon an outlook which I have had for many years. Long before the "cold war" began—during World War II when our country was an ally of the Soviet Union against Hitlerism— I pointed to certain new developments that would bring about a changed situation for my people. In an interview published in the New York *Times* on April 12, 1944, I said:

> "The problem of the Negro in this country is a very serious one. We in America criticize many nations. We know that international conscience has great influence in spite of wars. One important part of the solution of the Negro problem here will be the pressure of other countries on America from the outside. There are 100,000 Negroes now in the Army in the English theatre of operations. Americans wanted their segregation, as at home. The English, however, insisted upon their being mixed

in, without segregation. This shows the possibility of action within the Anglo-Saxon world, and it also shows the power of foreign opinion."

While pointing to the pressure from the outside, I was also convinced that the pressure from the Negro people themselves was also a factor that would have to be reckoned with, and I said so in these words:

"This is obviously not a race war—it turns, rather, on the idea of peoples that are free and those that are not free. The American Negro has changed his temper. Now he wants his freedom. Whether he is smiling at you or not, he wants his freedom. The old exploitation of peoples is definitely past."

That was my viewpoint more than a decade ago and that is my stand today.

I have outlined in this chapter the factors which, I believe, make it possible for Negro rights to be achieved at this time. But, as we well know, opportunity is not enough. No situation, however favorable, can solve a problem. "If there is no struggle," Douglass taught us, "there is no progress. Power concedes nothing without a demand. It never did and it never will." So let us next discuss the struggle that still must be waged, and the Negro power that can win our demand.

Chapter 5

THE POWER OF NEGRO ACTION

"How long, O Lord, how long?"—that ancient cry of the oppressed is often voiced these days in editorials in the Negro newspapers whose pages are filled with word-and-picture reports of outrages against our people. A photograph of a Negro being kicked by a white mobster brings the vicious blow crashing against the breast of the reader, and there are all the other horrible pictures—burning cross, beaten minister, bombed school, threatened children, mutilated man, imprisoned mother, barricaded family—which show what is going on.

How long? The answer is: *As long as we permit it.* I say that Negro action can be decisive. I say that we ourselves have the power to end the terror and to win for ourselves peace and security throughout the land. The recognition of this fact will bring new vigor, boldness and determination in planning our program of action and new militancy in winning its goals.

The denials and doubts about this idea—the second part of the challenge which confronts us today—are even more evident than those I noted in regard to the first. The diehard racists who shout "Never!" to equal rights, and the gradualists who mumble "Not now," are quite convinced that the Negro is powerless to bring about a different decision. Unfortunately, it is also true that to a large extent the Negro people do not know their own strength and do not see how they can achieve the goals they so urgently desire. The basis for this widespread view is obvious. We are a minority, a tenth of the population of our country. In all the terms in which power is reckoned in America—economic wealth, political office, social privilege—we are in a weak position; and from this the conclusion is drawn that the Negro can do little or nothing to compel a change.

It must be seen, however, that this is not a case of a minority pitting itself against a majority. If it were, if we wanted to gain something for ourselves by taking it away from the more powerful majority, the effort would plainly be hopeless. But that is not the case with our demand. Affirming that we are indeed created equal, we seek the equal rights to which we are entitled under the law. The granting of our demand would not lessen the democratic rights of the white people: on the contrary, it would enormously strengthen the base of democracy for all Americans. We ask for nothing that is not ours by right, and herein lies the great moral power of our demand. It is the admitted *rightness* of our claim which has earned for us the moral support of the majority of white Americans.

The granting of our demand for first-class citizenship, on a par with all others, would not in itself put us in a position of equality. Oppression has kept us on the bottom rungs of the ladder, and even with the removal of all barriers we will still have a long way to climb in order to catch up with the general standard of living. But the equal *place* to which we aspire cannot be reached without the equal *rights* we demand, and so the winning of those rights is not a maximum fulfillment but a minimum necessity and we cannot settle for less. Our viewpoint on this matter is not a minority opinion in our country. Though the most rabid champions of "white superiority" are unwilling to test their belief by giving the Negro an equal opportunity, I believe that most white Americans are fair-minded enough to concede that we should be given that chance.

The moral support of the American majority is largely passive today, but what must be recognized—and here we see the decisive power of Negro action—is this:

Wherever and whenever we, the Negro people, claim our lawful rights with all of the earnestness, dignity and determination that we can demonstrate, the moral support of the American people will become an active force on our side.

The most important part of the Little Rock story was not what Governor Faubus and the local mobs did, nor was it what President Eisenhower was moved to do: the important thing was that nine Negro youngsters, backed by their parents, the Negro community and its leadership, resolved to claim their right to attend Central High School. The magnificent courage and dignity these young people displayed in making that claim won the admiration of the American public. Their *action* did more to win the sympathy and support of democratic-minded white people than all the speeches about "tolerance" that have ever been made.

Little Rock was but one of the first skirmishes in the battle to end Jim Crow schools; much greater tests of our determination will soon be at hand. The desegregation of public education is as yet only in the first stages and the hard core of resistance has not been met. But there is no turning back, and the necessity to prepare ourselves for the struggles that lie ahead is urgent.

I have pointed to the sources of strength that exist at home and abroad. What power do we ourselves have?

We have the power of numbers, the power of organization, and the power of spirit. Let me explain what I mean.

Sixteen million people are a force to be reckoned with, and indeed there are many nations in the U.N. whose numbers are less. No longer can it be said that the Negro question is a sectional matter: the continuing exodus from the South has spread the Negro community to all parts of the land and has concentrated large numbers in places which are economically and politically the most important in the nation. In recent years much has been written about the strategic position of Negro voters in such pivotal states as New York, Ohio, Pennsylvania, Michigan, Illinois and California, but generally it can be said that the power of our numbers is not seen or acted upon. Let us consider this concept in connection with something that is apparent to all.

Very often these days we see photographs in the newspapers and magazines of a Negro family—the husband, wife, their children—huddled together in their newly purchased or rented home, while outside hundreds of Negro-haters have gathered to throw stones, to howl filthy abuse, to threaten murder and arson; and there may or may not be some policemen at the scene. But something is missing from this picture that ought to be there, and its absence gives rise to a nagging question that cannot be stilled: *Where are the other Negroes?* Where are the hundreds and thousands of other Negroes in that town who ought to be there protecting their own? The *power of numbers* that is missing from the scene would change the whole picture as nothing else could. It is one thing to terrorize a helpless few, but the forces of race hate that brazenly whoop and holler when the odds are a thousand to one are infinitely less bold when the odds are otherwise.

I am not suggesting, of course, that the Negro people should take law enforcement into their own hands. But we have the right and, above all, we have the duty, to bring the strength and support of our entire community to defend the lives and property of each individual family. Indeed, the law itself will move a hundred times quicker whenever it is apparent that the power of our numbers has been called forth. The time has come for the great Negro communities throughout the land—Chicago, Detroit, New York, Birmingham and all the rest—to demonstrate that they will no longer tolerate mob violence against one of their own. In listing the inalienable rights of man, Thomas Jefferson put *life* before *liberty, and the pursuit of happiness;* and it must be clear that for Negro Americans today the issue of *personal security* must be put first, and resolved first, before all other matters are attended to. When the Negro is told that he must "stay in his place," there is always the implicit threat that unless he does so mob violence will be used against him. Hence, as I see it, nothing is more important than to establish the fact that we will no longer suffer the use of mobs against us. Let the Negro people of but a single city respond in an all-out manner at the first sign of a mob—in mass demonstrations, by going on strike, by organizing boycotts—and the lesson will be taught in one bold stroke to people everywhere.

It was an excellent idea to call for a Prayer Pilgrimage for Freedom to assemble in Washington on May 17, 1957, the third anniversary of the Supreme Court decision, and the thousands who gathered there were inspired with a sense of solidarity and were deeply stirred by the speeches that were made. In terms of dignity and discipline the gathering was a matter for great pride. But there was at the same time a sense of disappointment at the size of the rally which did not, as a national mobilization, truly reflect the power of our numbers. Various charges were later made in the press, and heatedly denied, that important elements of leadership had "dragged their feet" in the preparations, but no constructive purpose would be served by going into those arguments here. The point I wish to make is this: When we call for such a mobilization again (and it ought to be done before another three years passes), we must go all-out to rally not tens of thousands but hundreds of thousands in a demonstration that will show we really mean business. And we should do more than listen to speeches and then go quietly home. Our spokesmen should go to the White House and to Congress and, backed by the massed power of our people, present our demands for action. Then they should come back to the assembled people to tell them what "the man" said, so that the people can decide whether they are satisfied or not and what to do about it.

The time for pussyfooting is long gone. If someone or other fears that some politician might be "embarrassed" by being confronted by such a delegation, or is concerned lest such action seem too bold—well, let that timid soul just step aside, for there are many in our ranks who will readily go in to "talk turkey" with any or all of the top men in government. We must get it into our heads—and into every leader's head—that we are not asking "favors" of the Big White Folks when, for example, we insist that the full power of the Executive be used to protect the right of Negroes to register and vote in the South. And when we really turn out for such a demand the answer can only be yes.

The *power of organization,* through which the power of numbers is expressed, is another great strength of the Negro people. Few other areas of American life are as intensively organized as is the Negro community. Some people say that we have far too many organizations—too many different churches and denominations, too many fraternal societies, clubs and associations—but that is what we have and there is no use deploring it. What is important is to recognize a meaningful fact which is so often denied: Negroes can and do band together and they have accomplished remarkable works through their collective efforts. "The trouble with our folks"—how often you have heard it (or perhaps said it yourself)—"is that we just won't get together"; but the plain truth is that we just about do more joining and affiliating than anybody else. "Our folks are just not ready to make financial sacrifices for a good cause," we hear, and yet we see that all over the country congregations of a few hundred poor people contribute and collect thousands of dollars year in and year out for the purposes that inspire them.

The Negro communities *are* organized and that condition is not made less significant by the fact that our people have formed a great number of organizations to meet their needs and desires. Organizations like the N.A.A.C.P., which has won many splendid victories in the courts for our rights and has done much other notable work, deserve a much greater membership and financial support than is now the case. Yet it is clear that to exert fully our power of organization we must bring together, for united action, all of the many organizations which now encompass the masses of our people. The great struggle and victory in Montgomery, Alabama, against Jim Crow buses proved beyond all doubt that the various existing organizations of the Negro community can be effectively united for a common purpose. Of course the factor of leadership, which I shall discuss later in this chapter, is a key point, but what I wish to emphasize here is that the *organizational base* for successful struggle exists in all other communities no less than in Montgomery. And who, in the face of the brilliant organization of every practical detail that was devised and carried through by our people in Montgomery, can still assert that Negroes do not have the capacity for effective collective action? What other mass movement in our country was better planned and carried out?

The central role that was played in Montgomery by the churches and their pastors highlights the fact that the Negro church, which has played such a notable part in our history, is still the strongest base of our power of organization. This is true not only because of the large numbers who comprise the congregations, but because our churches are, in the main, independent *Negro* organizations. The churches and other groups of similar independent character—fraternal orders, women's clubs, and so forth—will increasingly take the lead because they are closer to the Negro rank-and-file, more responsive to their needs, and less subject to control by forces outside the Negro community.

Here let me point to a large group among this rank-and-file which is potentially the most powerful and effective force in our community—the two million Negro men and women who are members of organized labor. We are a working people and the pay-envelope of the Negro worker is the measure of our general welfare and progress. Government statistics on average earnings show that for every dollar that the white worker is paid the Negro worker gets only 53 cents; and that the average Negro family has a yearly income of $2,410, compared with an average of $4,339 per year for white families. Here, on the basic bread-and-butter level, is a crucial front in our fight for equality and here the Negro trade unionists are the main force to lead the way.

It must be seen, too, that in relation to our general struggle for civil rights the Negro trade unionists occupy a key position. They comprise a large part of the membership of our community organizations and at the same time they are the largest section of our people belonging to interracial organizations. Hence, the Negro trade union members are a strategic link, a living connection with the great masses of the common people of America who are our natural allies in the struggle for democracy and whose active support must be won for our side in this critical hour.

To our men and women of organized labor I would say: A twofold challenge confronts you. The Negro trade unionists must increasingly exert their influence in every aspect of our people's community life. No church, no fraternal, civic or social organization in our communities must be permitted to continue without the benefit of the knowledge and experience that you have gained through your struggles in the great American labor movement. You are called upon to provide the spirit, the determination, the organizational skill, the firm steel of unyielding militancy to the age-old strivings of our people for equality and freedom.

Secondly, on your shoulders there is the responsibility to rally the strength of the whole trade union movement, white and black, to the battle for liberation of our people. Though you are still largely unrepresented in the top levels of labor leadership, you must use your power of numbers to see to it that the leadership of the A.F.L.-C.I.O., which has shown much concern for the so-called "crusade for freedom" abroad, shall not continue to be silent and unmoving in our crusade for freedom *at home*. You must rally your white fellow workers to support full equality for Negro workers; for their right to work at any job; to receive equal pay for equal work; for an end to Jim Crow unions; for the election of qualified Negroes to positions of union leadership; for fair employment practices in every industry; for trade union educational programs to eliminate the notions of "white superiority" which the employers use to poison the minds of the white workers in order to pit them against you.

I have watched and participated in your militant struggles everywhere I have been these past years—in Chicago with the packinghouse workers; with the auto workers of Detroit; the seamen and longshoremen of the West Coast; the tobacco workers of North Carolina; the miners of Pittsburgh and West Virginia; the steel workers of Illinois, Pennsylvania, Indiana and Ohio; the furriers, clerks and garment workers of New York and Philadelphia; with workers in numerous other places throughout the land—and I feel sure that you will meet the challenge which confronts you today.

To all groups in Negro life I would say that the key to set into motion our power of organization is the concept of *coordinated action,* the bringing together of the many organizations which exist in order to plan and to carry out the common struggle. We know full well that it is not easy to do this. We are divided in many ways—in politics, in religious affiliations, in economic and social classes; and in addition to these group rivalries there are the obstacles of personal ambitions and jealousies of various leaders. But as I move among our people these days, from New York to California, I sense a growing impatience with petty ways of thinking and doing things. I see a rising resentment against control of our affairs by white people, regardless of whether that domination is expressed by the blunt orders of political bosses or more discreetly by the "advice" of white liberals which must be heeded or else. There is a rapidly growing awareness that despite all of our differences it is necessary that we become unified, and I think that the force of that idea will overcome all barriers. Coordinated action will not, of course, come all at once: it will develop in the grass-roots and spread from community to community. And the building of that unity is a task which each of us can undertake wherever we are.

A unified people requires a unified leadership, and let me make very clear what I mean by that. Recently the distinguished Negro journalist Carl T. Rowan, who had published in *Ebony* magazine an interview with me, was himself interviewed about that subject on a radio network program where he said: "It's Robeson's contention that the Negro people will never be free in this country until they speak more or less as one voice, and, very obviously, Robeson feels that that one voice should be something close to his voice."

Actually, that is *not* how I feel, and I would not want Mr. Rowan or anyone else to misunderstand my view of this matter. The one voice in which we should speak must be the expression of our entire people on the central issue which is all-important to every Negro—our right to be free and equal. On many other issues there are great differences among us, and hence it is not possible for any one person, or any group of people, to presume to speak for us all.

Far from making any such claim for myself, what I am advocating is in fact the opposite idea! I advocate a unity based upon our common viewpoint as Negroes, a nonpartisan unity, a unity in which we subordinate all that divides us, a unity which excludes no one, a unity in which no faction or group is permitted to impose its particular outlook on others. A unified leadership of a unified movement means that people of *all* political views—conservatives, liberals, and radicals—must be represented therein. Let there be but one requirement made without exception: that Negro leadership, and every man and woman in that leadership, place the interests of our people, and the struggle for those interests, above all else.

There is a need—an urgent need—for a national conference of Negro leadership, not of a handful but a broad representative gathering of leadership from all parts of the country, from all walks of life, from every viewpoint, to work out a *common program of action* for Negro Americans in the crisis of our times. Such a program does not exist today and without it we are a ship without a rudder; we can only flounder around on a day-to-day basis, trying to meet developments with patchwork solutions. We must chart a course to be followed in the stormy days that are here and in the greater storms that are on the way, a course that heads full square for freedom.

The need for a *central fund*, not only for legal purposes but for all the purposes of Negro coordinated action, has been expressed in various editorials in the press and elsewhere; and the national conference I speak of could meet this need. A central fund would be a "community chest" to help our struggles everywhere. Nonpartisan and not controlled by any single organization, this fund would be a national institution of our whole people, and a well-organized campaign to build it would meet with a generous response from Negro America. And more: such a fund would undoubtedly receive a great deal of support from white people who sympathize with our struggle.

If we must think boldly in terms of the power of numbers, we must likewise think big in terms of organization. Our cause is the cause of all, and so our methods of reaching our goal must be such that all of our people can play a part. The full potential of the Negro people's power of organization must be achieved in every city and state throughout the land.

The *power of spirit* that our people have is intangible, but it is a great force that must be unleashed in the struggles of today. A spirit of steadfast determination, exaltation in the face of trials—it is the very soul of our people that has been formed through all the long and weary years of our march toward freedom. It is the deathless spirit of the great ones who have led our people in the past—Douglass, Tubman and all the others—and of the millions who kept "a-inching along." That spirit lives in our people's songs—in the sublime grandeur of "Deep River," in the driving power of "Jacob's Ladder," in the militancy of "Joshua Fit the Battle of Jericho," and in the poignant beauty of all our spirituals.

It lives in every Negro mother who wants her child "to grow up and be somebody," as it lives in our common people everywhere who daily meet insult and outrage with quiet courage and optimism. It is that spirit which gives that "something extra" to our athletes, to our artists, to all who meet the challenge of public performance. It is the spirit of little James Gordon of Clay, Kentucky, who, when asked by a reporter why he wanted to go to school with white children, replied: "Why shouldn't I?"; and it is the spirit of all the other little ones in the South who have walked like mighty heroes through menacing mobs to go to school. It is the spirit of the elderly woman of Montgomery who explained her part in the bus boycott by saying: "When I rode in the Jim Crow buses my body was riding but my soul was walking, but now when my body is walking my soul is riding!"

Yes, that power of the spirit is the pride and glory of my people, and there is no human quality in all of America that can surpass it. It is a force only for good: there is no hatefulness about it. It exalts the finest things of life—justice and equality, human dignity and fulfillment. It is of the earth, deeply rooted, and it reaches up to the highest skies and mankind's noblest aspirations. It is time for this spirit to be evoked and exemplified in all we do, for it is a force mightier than all our enemies and will triumph over all their evil ways.

For Negro action to be decisive—given the favorable opportunity which I have outlined in the previous chapter and the sources of strength indicated above—still another factor is needed: *effective Negro leadership*. In discussing this subject I shall not engage in any personalities, nor is it my intention either to praise or blame the individuals who today occupy top positions in our ranks. Such critical appraisal must, of course, be made of their leaders by the Negro people, and so I would like here to discuss not this or that person but rather the *principles* of the question, the standards for judgment, the character of leadership that is called for today.

The term "leadership" has been used to express many different concepts, and many of these meanings have nothing to do with what I am concerned with here. Individuals attain prominence for a wide variety of reasons, and often people who have climbed up higher on the ladder are called leaders though they make it plain that their sole interest is personal advancement and the more elevated they are above all other Negroes the better they like it. Then, too, it has been traditional for the dominant group of whites, in local communities and on a national scale as well, to designate certain individuals as "Negro leaders," regardless of how the Negro people feel about it; and the idea is that Negro leadership is something that white folks can bestow as a favor or take away as punishment.

The concept that I am talking about has nothing to do with matters of headline prominence, personal achievement, or popularity with the powers-that-be. I am concerned, rather, with Negro leadership in the struggle for Negro rights. This includes those who are directly in charge of the organizations established for such purpose, and many others as well—the leaders of Negro churches, fraternal and civic organizations, elected representatives in government, trade union officials, and others whose action or inaction directly affects our common cause.

The primary quality that Negro leadership must possess, as I see it, is *a single-minded dedication to their people's welfare.* Any individual Negro, like any other person, may have many varied interests in life, but for the true leader all else must be subordinated to the interests of those whom he is leading. If today it can be said that the Negro people of the United States are lagging behind the progress being made by colored peoples in other lands, one basic cause for it has been that all too often Negro leadership here has lacked the selfless passion for their people's welfare that has characterized the leaders of the colonial liberation movements. Among us there is a general recognition—and a grudging acceptance—of the fact that some of our leaders are not only unwilling to make sacrifices but they must see some gain for themselves in whatever they do. A few crumbs for a few is too often hailed as "progress for the race." To live in freedom one must be prepared to die to achieve it, and while few if any of us are ever called upon to make that supreme sacrifice, no one can ignore the fact that in a difficult struggle those who are in the forefront may suffer cruel blows. He who is not prepared to face the trials of battle will never lead to a triumph. This spirit of dedication, as I have indicated, is abundantly present in the ranks of our people but progress will be slow until it is much more manifest in the character of leadership.

Dedication to the Negro people's welfare is one side of a coin: the other side is *independence*. Effective Negro leadership must rely upon and be responsive to no other control than the will of their people. We have allies—important allies—among our white fellow-citizens, and we must ever seek to draw them closer to us and to gain many more. But the Negro people's movement must be led by *Negroes*, not only in terms of title and position but in reality. Good advice is good no matter what the source and help is needed and appreciated from wherever it comes, but Negro action cannot be decisive if the advisers and helpers hold the guiding reins. For no matter how well-meaning other groups may be, the fact is our interests are secondary at best with them.

Today such outside controls are a factor in reducing the independence and effectiveness of Negro leadership. I do not have in mind the dwindling group of Uncle Toms who shamelessly serve even an Eastland; happily, they are no longer of much significance. I have in mind, rather, those practices of Negro leadership that are based upon the idea that it is white power rather than Negro power that must be relied upon. This concept has been traditional since Booker T. Washington, and it has been adhered to by many who otherwise reject all notions of white supremacy. Even Marcus Garvey, who rose to leadership of a nationalist mass movement in the 1920's and who urged that the Negro peoples of the world "go forward to the point of destiny as laid out by themselves," believed that white power was decisive. Indeed, no one has stated the idea more clearly than Garvey did in his essay "The Negro's Place in World Reorganization," in which he said:

> "The white man of America has become the natural leader of the world. He, because of his exalted position,

is called upon to help in all human efforts. From nations to individuals the appeal is made to him for aid in all things affecting humanity, so, naturally, there can be no great mass movement or change without first acquainting the leader on whose sympathy and advice the world moves."

Much has changed since those words were written, and I have no doubt that if Garvey were alive today he would recognize that the "white man of America" is no longer all-powerful and that the colored peoples of the world are moving quite independently of that "sympathy and advice."

In Booker Washington's day it was the ruling white man of the South whose sympathy was considered indispensable; today it is the liberal section of the dominant group in the North whose goodwill is said to be the hope for Negro progress. It is clear that many Negro leaders act or desist from acting because they base themselves on this idea. Rejecting the concept that "white is right" they embrace its essence by conceding that "might is right." To the extent that this idea is prevalent in its midst, Negro leadership lacks the quality of independence without which it cannot be effective.

Dedication and independence—these are the urgent needs. Other qualities of leadership exist in abundance: we have many highly trained men and women, experienced in law, in politics, in civic affairs; we have spokesmen of great eloquence, talented organizers, skilled negotiators. If I have stressed those qualities which are most needed on the national level, it is not from any lack of appreciation for much that is admirable. On the local level, especially, there are many examples of dedicated and independent leadership. Indeed, the effective use of Negro power—of numbers, of organization, of spirit—in Montgomery was the result of Negro leadership of the highest caliber. And the whole nation has witnessed the heroic dedication of many other leaders in the South, who, at the risk of their lives and all they hold dear, are leading their people's struggles. There are many from our ranks who ought to be elevated to national leadership because by their deeds they have fully demonstrated their right to be there.

We should broaden our conception of leadership and see to it that all sections of Negro life are represented on the highest levels. There must be room at the top for people from down below. I'm talking about the majority of our folks who work in factory and field: they bring with them that down-to-earth view which is the highest vision, and they can hammer and plow in more ways than one. Yes, we need more of them in the leadership, and we need them in a hurry.

We need more of our women in the higher ranks, too, and who should know better than the children of Harriet Tubman, Sojourner Truth and Mary Church Terrell that our womenfolk have often led the way. Negro womanhood today is giving us many inspiring examples of steadfast devotion, cool courage under fire, and brilliant generalship in our people's struggles; and here is a major source for new strength and militancy in Negro leadership on every level.

But if there are those who ought to be raised to the top, there are some others already there who should be retired. I have noted, in another connection, that the Negro people are patient and long-suffering—sometimes to a fault. The fault is often expressed by permitting unworthy leaders to get away with almost anything. It is as if once a man rises to leadership, his responsibility to his people is no longer binding upon him.

But, in these critical days, we ought to become a little less tolerant, a little more demanding that all Negro leaders "do right." I have in mind, for example, the case of an important Negro leader in a large Northern city, who, at the time when mobs were barring the Negro children from high school in Little Rock and beating up Negro newspapermen, got up before his people and said: "We cannot meet this crisis by force against force. Under no circumstances can Federal troops be used. This would be a confession of our moral decadence, it would precipitate a second Civil War—it would open the stopper and send democracy down the drain for at least our generation and maybe forever." These words, so utterly devoid of any concern for his people and lacking all regard for the truth, were hardly spoken before the President sent in Federal troops! No civil war was started, democracy got a new lease on life, the mobs were dispersed, the Negro children were escorted to school, and for the first time since 1876 the lawful force of the Federal government was called out against the lawless force of White Supremacy in the South.

When, as in this case, a Negro leader vigorously opposes that which he should be fighting for and makes it clear that some other folks' interests are of more concern to him than his own people's—well, the so-called "politically-wise" may say: "Oh, that's just politics—forget it." But the so-called "politically-dumb" just can't see it that way. How can we be led by people who are not going our way?

There are others, honest men beyond all doubt and sincerely concerned with their people's welfare, who seem to feel that it is the duty of a leader to discourage Negro mass action. They think that best results can be achieved by the quiet negotiations they carry on. And so when something happens that arouses the masses of people, and when the people gather in righteous anger to demand that militant actions be started, such men believe it their duty to cool things off.

We saw this happen not long ago when from coast to coast there was a great upsurge of the people caused by the brutal lynching of young Emmett Till. At one of the mass protest meetings that was held, I heard one of our most important leaders address the gathering in words to this effect: "You are angry today, but you are not going to do anything about it. I know that you won't do anything. You clamor for a march on Mississippi but none of you will go. So let's stop talking about marching. Just pay a dollar to our organization and leave the rest to your leaders. If you want to do something yourself, let each of you go to your district Democratic leader and talk to him about it."

Well, what would a congregation think of their pastor if the best he could do was to tell them: "You are all a bunch of sinners, and nothing can make you do right. There is no good in you and I know it. So, brothers and sisters, just put your contributions on the collection plate, go home and leave your salvation to me."

No, a leader should encourage, not discourage; he should rally the people, not disperse them. A wet blanket can never be the banner of freedom.

Of course there must be negotiations made in behalf of our rights, but unless the negotiators are backed by an aroused and militant people, their earnest pleas will be of little avail. For Negro action to be effective—to be decisive, as I think it can be—it must be *mass* action. The power of the ballot can be useful only if the masses of voters are united on a common program; obviously, if half the Negro people vote one way and the other half the opposite way, not much can be achieved. The individual votes are cast and counted, but the group power is cast away and discounted.

Mass action—in political life and elsewhere—is Negro power in motion; and it is the way to win.

An urgent task which faces us today is an all-out struggle to defeat the efforts of the White Supremacists to suppress the N.A.A.C.P. in the South. As in South Africa, where the notorious "Suppression of Communism Act" is used to attack the liberation movement, the enemies of Negro freedom in our country have accused the N.A.A.C.P. of being a "subversive conspiracy" and the organization has been outlawed in Louisiana, Texas and Alabama, and legally restricted in Georgia, Virginia, South Carolina and Mississippi. City ordinances, as in Little Rock, are also used for this purpose.

The indifference with which various other organizations viewed the suppression in 1955 of the Council on African Affairs,* which was falsely labeled a "Communist front," should not be repeated now by any group in the case of the

---

* See Appendix D, page 118, for a summary of the record of the Council on African Affairs prepared by W. Alphaeus Hunton. Dr. Hunton, after 17 years on the faculty of Howard University, served from 1943 to 1955 as educational director and later as executive secretary of the Council. His recent book, *Decision in Africa* (International Publishers, New York, 1957), is an invaluable source for the truth about Africa today.

N.A.A.C.P. The Red-baiting charges against that organization are utterly untrue, as the makers of such charges know full well; and those elements in Negro leadership who have in the past resorted to Red-baiting as a "smart" tactic should realize that such methods serve no one but our people's worst enemies.

Throughout the South—in Little Rock, in Montgomery and elsewhere—the state and local leaders of the N.A.A.C.P. have set a heroic and inspiring example for Negro leadership everywhere. All of us—the Negro people of the entire country—must rally now to sustain and defend them.

In presenting these ideas on the power of Negro action, the sources of that power, and the character of leadership necessary to direct that power most effectively, I offer them for consideration and debate at this time when the challenge of events calls for clarity of vision and unity of action. No one, obviously, has all the answers, and the charting of our course must be done collectively. There must be a spirit of give and take, and clashing viewpoints must find a common ground. Partisan interests must be subordinated to Negro interests—by each of us. Somehow we must find the way to set aside all that divides us and come together, Negroes all. Our unity will strengthen our friends and win many more to our side; and our unity will weaken our foes who already can see the handwriting on the wall.

To be free—to walk the good American earth as equal citizens, to live without fear, to enjoy the fruits of our toil, to give our children every opportunity in life—that dream which we have held so long in our hearts is today the destiny that we hold in our hands.

Epilogue

OUR CHILDREN, OUR WORLD

In the glow of lamplight on my desk I gaze upon one of the wondrous signs of our times, full of hope and promise for the future . . . and I smile to see in these newspaper photographs the faces, so bright, so solemn, of our young heroes—the children of Little Rock. Their names are: *Elizabeth Eckford, Carlotta Walls, Minnie Jean Brown, Gloria Ray, Thelma Mothershed, Melba Patillo, Jefferson Thomas, Terrence Roberts,* and *Ernest Green.* And to the list could be added the names of all the other Negro children in the Southland who have given us great new epics of courage and dignity. The patter of their feet as they walk through Jim Crow barriers to attend school is the thunder of the marching men of Joshua, and the world rocks beneath their tread.

Dear children of Little Rock—you and your parents and the Negro people of your community have lifted our hearts and renewed our resolve that full freedom shall now be ours. You are the pride and the glory of our people, and my heart sings warm and tender with love for you. Our country will never be truly great and good until you and all the rest of our young people are permitted to flower in complete fulfillment and bring your gifts to the highest levels of our nation's life.

You are our children, but the peoples of the whole world rightly claim you, too. They have seen your faces, and the faces of those who hate you, and they are on *your* side. They see in you those qualities which parents everywhere want their children to have, and their best wishes—the love of all good people for children—goes out to you.

Yes, America—these are your children, too, and you ought to be very proud of them. The American dream—the spirit of Jefferson and Lincoln, of Emerson and Twain—is given new life by the children of Little Rock. These children must ever be cherished, for they are not only the hope and the promise of my people: with them stands the destiny of democracy in America.

. . . I look up from my desk and gaze out through the tall windows of my room to the sky over Harlem, and I reflect upon still another wondrous sign of our times. Up there in the heavens the stars blink with astonishment to see that old Mother Earth has a couple of brand new children—the little man-made moons that merrily race around her. And I smile again to know that somewhere far overhead the sputniks are rushing by, tracing out the great truth for the whole world to see: *There are no heights which mankind cannot scale!* And I think of my friends, the peoples of the Soviet Union, whose hands and brains have fashioned this miracle which opens up the limitless horizons of space to earth-bound Man.

When the first wheel was made, when the first book was printed, there were those who saw in the new inventions some kind of a threat and a menace; and today there are prophets of gloom in our land who say that the sputniks represent a danger to our country. Nonsense! This is a triumph for the whole human race, a great new breakthrough of science and technology which are the tools for a better life for us all. No doubt there are some brink-of-war statesmen and some jingoistic generals who have heard in the "beep beep" of the sputniks a message to themselves—"Little men, you'd better forget your crazy plans for war!"—and if that is the way they understand it, it's all to the good.

Wise men and fools alike can see that a new star of peace has arisen in the East: Sputnik tells us all that war is indeed unthinkable, and that the nations of the earth must find the way to peaceful coexistence—especially the United States and the Union of Soviet Socialist Republics whose friendship would guarantee peace for all the world.

The Negro newspapers on my desk are filled with my people's thoughts as they see these signs of our times—Little Rock and little moon. In editorials and letters to the editor they point to the menace they see and feel: the enemy is *racism*, and they brand that enemy as the foe of human progress. Sputnik, they say, was produced by a school system which includes people of all races, and they charge that Jim Crow practices here, which bar most Negro children from an equal education, are also a barrier in America's path to new heights of scientific achievement.

So, hello up there, little Sputnik—thanks a million for the message my people have gotten from you! I'm sure it is going to do us a lot of good.

Peace—yes, that is the all-important thing. With peace assured, all nations and races will flower. Soon, when Man travels the paths blazed by these little moons, he will look down upon our Mother Earth and say, with great love and pride for all mankind, what Shakespeare said of his homeland: "This happy breed of men, this little world. . . ."

And I think of a great poet of the Americas in our own day, Pablo Neruda of Chile, who in the closing lines of his epic poem "Let the Rail-Splitter Awake," speaks also for me:

> *Let us think of the entire earth*
> *and pound the table with love.*
> *I don't want blood again*
> *to saturate bread, beans, music:*
> *I wish they would come with me:*
> *the miner, the little girl,*
> *the lawyer, the seaman,*
> *the doll-maker,*
> *to go into a movie and come out*
> *to drink the reddest wine . . .*
> *I came here to sing*
> *and for you to sing with me.*

APPENDIX

A.

My Brother, Paul

By Rev. Benjamin C. Robeson

The family had just finished dinner, the day was hot and sultry. We began to lounge comfortably in our common den, when suddenly Bill suggested that we strike up a few tunes. We started out with gusto, Bill, Paul and I. "Down by the Old Mill Stream" was the ballad of the day. After touching it off, we gradually went through our repertoire which touched everything from "Turkey in the Straw" to "Silent Night." We were making one of those minors known only to home-loving groups; Paul was bearing down on it with boyish glee; in fact, all of us were. Out of all the discord, Bill yelled: "Wait a minute, hit that note again, Paul." Paul hit it out of the lot, and Bill said: "Paul, you can sing."

"Stop kidding me, boy."

"My musical education has been sadly neglected," said Bill. "But Paul, good music sounds good, just like good food tastes good. You can sing, but just to be sure that we have no accident, when we return tonight I want you to sing 'Annie Laurie.' If you satisfy me, the Robeson manse will issue its first musical diploma."

We broke for a baseball game in the lots, which was the perfect end to every fair day. Upon returning home, we settled for the night (strange to say, most of them were always spent at the homestead). Bill called for his selection. His memory was tenacious; he forgot nothing. Paul had to satisfy him to have any peace. Bill listened as he warbled, and concluded: "Paul, you *can* sing."

Of course, Paul thought it a joke, and I voted with him. Singing was the last talent of the Robeson family, according to our judgment. Father had kept it all, we long ago decided.

As to Paul's singing, however, a number of circumstances gradually forced Paul to the conviction that there might be a grain of truth in Bill's contention. He gave himself with more attention to helping the choir at church. Entertainments were always numerous, and the law of the parsonage was that every child must do something. The rest of us had recourse to nothing but a recitation or essay, and Paul, to be different, was forced to sing. From this to the Glee Club in high school he went, until finally he was at least partially satisfied that he could sing. Still, the idea of branching out into concert work was not even an embryonic thought. Whatever he does today in the line of singing started that July afternoon, with Bill, Paul and myself. Without that happening, I doubt if he would ever have been near any singing group.

Bill sleeps today in his grave, harboring the unrealized ambitions of his heart in the medical profession; but, the more I think of it, he wrought better than he knew. Paul is medicine to me—the music of his soul has cured me of many maladies. Bill was practicing medicine with an uncanny vision when he made his diagnosis and prescribed that course of treatment.

Mother gave us much—a queen in the realm of an education which carried all of its power into the spiritual region. She wrote as many sermons as Father, and as I gaze upon them today, I often wonder how she did it; how she could so uncannily frame those gems of thought and feeling. She gave us an inflow of Quaker blood, with all of its spiritual propensities. Its outworking seems to have been more pronounced in Marion, Paul and myself. I attribute this to the fact that, when we drew near, she was suffering greatly from the impairment of her eyesight and, as always, suffering tends to touch the depths and bring to the surface the finest that we have.

To understand Paul, one must know this. He moves by his inner revelations. Experience has taught him to do this. He never fails, is never disappointed or perplexed when he follows his flash. He is at perfect ease moving this way. In a moment he senses everything; he asks every question that comes to the normal mind, and answer or no answer, he obeys his flash.

In early youth he decided to take the ministry. Father's death, the war with its shattering of dreams, plunged him into the depths of something he is just now beginning to fathom. Who would dare assert that he is not in the ministry? His singing and acting just happen to be the means of his livelihood. He is bearing the cross of a despised, oppressed and neglected people; he is voicing the heartaches of the years that he has seen—and the memories of his father rehearsing the flight through blood and tears via the Underground Railroad to the rostrum of freedom where he could proclaim what he knew was "good news."

Have you heard Paul sing "Witness"? He is there the personification of his father with his own personality added. He is singing then for his Lord and Master; for while he may not be orthodox when it comes to church attendance, he believes and knows to whom he has committed his all. Here lies the heart of his singing and acting, too. He visions himself breaking down the barriers that have imprisoned his race for centuries. He knows that hidden away in the teeming millions of African extraction there are others who, if favored by fortune, would be out there in the swim, making a healthy contribution to the progress of humanity.

His vision only begins there: he sees how blind and unreasonable prejudice is, in all of its forms; how it has its grip on the world and at every crossroad, whether it is national or international matters.

struggles to choke and stifle the finest and best within us all. The ditch-digger who glorifies his job can thrill Paul much quicker than a learned scientist, obeying rigidly the law of facts and forever refusing to take off his shoes in their presence. The personality striving to explore the outer reaches of his horizon, and then expand it soulfully, can grip Paul's attention any time, whether he be Bert Williams in his inimitable field or Chaliapin who walks the heights with the immortals.

B.

(An excerpt from the address of Dr. Benjamin E. Mays, President of Morehouse College, on the occasion of the award to Mr. Robeson of the honorary degree of Doctor of Humane Letters, June 1, 1943.)

"You, perhaps more than any other person, have made Negro music accepted as first-rate art by the world at large. You have rendered the Negro race and the world a great service in *Othello* by demonstrating that Negroes are capable of great and enduring interpretations in the realm of the theatre as over against the typical cheap performances that Hollywood and Broadway too often insist on Negroes doing.

"You have had the courage to dignify and popularize the folk-songs composed by the oppressed peoples of the earth. You have proved that you have a mission in song and a deep, abiding faith in that mission. In your singing you champion the cause of the common man. Whether it is a Negro spiritual, the folk-song of France, or Canada, the songs of the Mexican peons, the Jew's longing for release from persecution, the brave chant of the Russian soldier, the songs of Madrid at the time of bombardment, or a song portraying the heroism of London and China, you, Mr. Robeson, embody in your person the sufferings of mankind.

"Your singing is a declaration of faith. You sing as if God Almighty sent you into the world to advocate the cause of the common man in song. You are truly the people's artist.

"In your search for freedom you experience a common bond between the suffering and oppressed folks of the world, that folk music is universal and that folks are alike everywhere. It is quite possible that there is not and perhaps there never will be again in this generation a folk singer your equal.

"You have the genius of touching the hearts of men, whether they walk the highway of kings or tread the lowly path of peasants. You have thrilled the hearts of thousands in song and in picture and in drama. You have given hope to and warmed the hearts of the oppressed millions in every land. You represent in your person, in your integrity, and in your ideals the things for which the college stands and for which it shall continue to stand.

"We are happy, therefore, to be the first Negro college in the world to place its stamp of approval upon the leadership of a man who embodies all the hopes and aspirations of the Negro race and who, despite crippling restrictions, breathes the pure air of freedom."

C.

A Universal Body of Folk Music — A Technical Argument by the Author

During the recent years of my enforced professional immobilization, I have found enormous satisfaction in exploring the origins and interrelations of various folk musics, and have come to some interesting and challenging ideas—supported by many world renowned musicologists—which further confirm and explain my own and Lawrence Brown's interest in and attraction to the world body of folk music.

Continued study and research into the origins of the folk music of various peoples in many parts of the world revealed that there is a world body—a universal body—of folk music based upon a universal pentatonic (five tone) scale. Interested as I am in the universality of mankind—in the fundamental relationship of all peoples to one another—this idea of a universal body of music intrigued me, and I pursued it along many fascinating paths.

My people, the Negro people of America, have been reared on the pentatonic scale and pentatonic melodies, in Africa and in America. No wonder Lawrence Brown introduced me to the music of Moussorgsky (of the Russian "Five"); to the music of Dvorak and Janacek; to ancient Hebraic chants; to the old melodies of Scotland and Ireland; to the Flamenco and de Falla of Spain; to the music of Armenia, and of Albania, Bulgaria, Rumania, Hungary and Poland, especially to the songs of Kodaly and Bartok; the music of contemporary Soviet composers; to the music of ancient Africa; to S. Coleridge Taylor; to the music of Ethiopia; the melodies of Brazil and of the Caribbean—based as they are on African rhythm and melody; to the music of the North and South American Indian peoples. And I have found my way to the music of China, of Central Asia, Mongolia, of Indonesia, Viet Nam and of India.

And always, with my "pentatonic ears," my interest in the fundamental five-tone scale grew. J. Rosamond Johnson's comments on African and Afro-American music are extremely interesting in this connection. In his book, *Rolling Along in Song* (Viking Press, N. Y., 1937) he writes:

"The Negro hesitated, pondered for a while, and then with fond affection hung his banjo on the wall and found the inspiration for a new style of rhythm simply by pounding on the black keys of the piano. His native instinct had led him into the pentatonic scale.

Staying on the black keys, he found easily the five-tone formula so distinctively characteristic of African music."

Very interesting and illuminating in this connection, are Marion Bauer's comments on the pentatonic in her book, *Twentieth Century Music* (G. P. Putnam's Sons, New York and London, 1947):

"The pentatonic, which may be found by playing the black keys on the piano, was doubtless a universal scale, not belonging to any one nation or race, but marking a stage in the evolution of man's consciousness. The Chinese and Japanese have clung to it throughout the centuries; it is familiar to us through many characteristic Scotch and Irish folk songs; traces of the pentatonic are to be found in the music of the American Indians and Eskimos, as well as in that of the Africans."

It is very interesting to note that in recent years many Western composers have turned to their old pentatonic modal folk music, finding new inspiration in this wealth and basing many of their new compositions upon it, just as Bach based much of his music on the ancient modal folk Chorales. These composers have found richness in pentatonic modal melodies because, as Joseph Yasser conclusively demonstrates, there is also a *pentatonic harmony* which has long existed and been developed in China, Africa, Indonesia, etc., and in Europe up to 1500. That is to say, there is a pentatonic system of music which preceded and co-exists with the better known diatonic or seven-tone system—the one in general use in the classic music of Europe after 1700. However, this pentatonic system has always continued in folk music. My dear friend and colleague Lawrence Brown has also drawn upon this richness, and has made many beautiful arrangements of our own folk music. And as Kodaly and Bartok point out and conclusively demonstrate, their harmony is drawn from the inner logic of the pentatonic modal melodies.

In *Musical Form* (Harvard University Press, 1951), Hugo Leichtentritt says of Bartok:

"Among modern composers, Bela Bartok has, more than anybody else, exploited unusual scales and strange harmonic effects derived from them . . . in the 'Allegro barbaro' for piano he uses a scale composed of C major and F sharp minor-major plus the same scale a fifth higher—G major and C sharp minor-major. . . . Here is seen a nine or sometimes even a ten-tone scale."

Bartok himself gives a real clue in his *Microcosmos* (Vol. 2), written for children, entitled "Two Major Pentachords," precisely on C and F sharp. So the scale could be looked at as two contrasting pentatonics, providing a kind of natural folk-song bi-tonality. This gives Bartok's work a very advanced and modern harmonic feeling.

If children, who learn their modal and pentatonic melodies at an early age, could be taught to look at the piano as comprised of two pentatonic scales, or two folk songs (with two auxiliary tones common to each scale), it might shorten the time of instruction and ease the work load for them. Each pentatonic is in itself a folk tune. Since this musical language is as much a part of children as their spoken tongue, they might be taught to experiment with these two pentatonics and with their interrelationships, especially the *tri-tone* relationship.

It may well be that today, after many fascinating and rewarding digressions, we are flowing back into the mainstream of world music—which includes the music of Asia, Africa, Europe and the Americas—with a future potential of immense musical wealth, all giving to and taking from each other through this wonderful world bank of music.

D.

A Note on the Council on African Affairs

By W. ALPHAEUS HUNTON

The work of the Council on African Affairs, Paul Robeson stated publicly on more than one occasion, was the one organizational interest among many with which he was identified that was closest to his heart. He was instrumental in the establishment of the Council in 1937 and for eighteen years, until its dissolution in 1955, was intimately associated with its activities, serving most of that time as the organization's chairman. His unswerving devotion to the cause of African freedom, his world-encompassing vision, and his powerful voice and big human spirit were of inestimable importance in forwarding the Council's efforts toward rallying Americans, black and white, in support of Africa's liberation from imperialist bondage.

One reflection of the Africans' recognition and appreciation of his great service was the selection of Paul Robeson as one of three recipients—together with Kwame Nkrumah, now Prime Minister of free Ghana, and Nnamdi Azikiwe, Prime Minister of Eastern Nigeria—of the award of "Champion of African Freedom," bestowed by the National Church of Nigeria at ceremonies attended by 5,000 at Aba, Nigeria, on January 29, 1950.

The Council on African Affairs for many years stood alone as the one organization in the United States devoting full-time attention to the problems and struggles of the peoples of Africa.

No detailed account of the Council's work can be given here, but it may be helpful to say something briefly about its major functions. Its prime objective was to provide a sound basis of accurate information so that the American people might play their proper part in the struggle for African freedom. To that end, the Council serviced the press with African news and background information; provided speakers, films, and exhibit materials wherever requested; published a monthly bulletin of information and comment on African developments; circulated numerous pamphlets and factual reports; and maintained an extensive African library and research facilities.

Though the dissemination of information was central in its work, the Council was not content to function simply as an information agency. It sought to translate knowledge into action. From 1944 when the shape of postwar African policy was under consideration to 1955 and Bandung, the Council organized assemblies ranging from conferences of community leaders to a Madison Square Garden rally for the purpose of hammering out, and enlisting public support for, programs of action in the interest of the African peoples' welfare and freedom.

Beginning with the founding conference of the United Nations in San Francisco the Council maintained a close watch on the activities and policies of the world organization pertaining to Africa and colonial countries in general. It brought to public attention and helped generate protests against the pro-imperialist and compromising stand of the United States delegation on such issues as trusteeship and colonial independence, the status of South West Africa, the question of Italy's former colonies in Africa, and the tyranny of racist rule in the Union of South Africa. "The knowledge that we have friends at the other end of the Atlantic is comforting and inspiring in our struggle for freedom from want and heartless exploitation," a Nigerian trade union leader wrote the Council's officers.

Another facet of the Council's work, an area of activity in which its influence was perhaps most effective and widespread, pertained to campaigns to provide direct assistance for Africans in emergency situations. The significance of one of these campaigns has been described by Dr. Z. K. Matthews, a distinguished educator and a leader of the African National Congress in South Africa, and one of the 156 men and women placed on trial there for "treason" in 1957 when the Strijdom regime launched an all-out assault on the vanguard of the forces striving for democratic rights.

Writing from South Africa in 1953, Dr. Matthews said of the Council, "Africans in this country have benefited directly from its practical interest in their affairs. As far back as 1945 when a severe drought struck the Eastern Cape Province of the Union of South Africa, hundreds of Africans . . . had cause to be thankful that such a body as the Council on African Affairs was in existence. . . . The Council made available financial aid and food supplies of various kinds collected in America to be forwarded to the area for distribution among the needy. Many African children, women and older people in the area concerned owed their lives to the assistance given by the Council."

It was in relation to this campaign that the late Senator Harley M. Kilgore in 1946 declared: "The Council on African Affairs deserves the wholehearted support of every American for its great fight to secure freedom and full democratic rights for the oppressed and starving South Africans and other colonial peoples. . . . Every American who supports the Council's drive to aid the starving South Africans will be striking a solid blow for world freedom."

But two years later came the official branding of the Council as "subversive" and the descent of the McCarthyite blanket of fear and suspicion smothering all free democratic expression. Nevertheless, despite heavy obstacles, the work went on and further campaigns were organized to provide financial aid to help defray the expenses of the legal defense of Jomo Kenyatta and other leaders of the Kenya African Union charged with conspiring with the Mau Mau, and to provide for the support of the dependents of the thousands of men and women jailed in South Africa during the Campaign of Defiance of Unjust Laws.

There was also the work of the African Aid Committee, headed by Dr. W. E. B. Du Bois, who was elected as Vice Chairman of the Council in 1949. Among this Committee's accomplishments was the collection and forwarding of funds to aid the families of 26 miners shot down during a strike in the coal pits of Enugu, Nigeria.

Such, in brief, were the main features of the work of the Council on African Affairs. Though the organization was ultimately forced to suspend its activities, what it achieved could not be undone. Today, with Africa's millions demonstrating their determination to manage their own affairs for their own benefit, there is growing realization of the folly of continuing to give European or American economic and strategic objectives in that continent priority over African self-determination and emancipation.

E.

A Later Statement by the Author

(*Four months after the publication of* Here I Stand, *Paul Robeson won his long struggle to regain his passport; and in July, 1958, he resumed his stage and concert career abroad. A protracted illness, beginning in 1961, forced his retirement from public life; and he returned to his home in New York in December, 1963. In Robeson's first public statement after his return—a release to the Negro press—he commented on the changes that had occurred in the black community in the seven years since he wrote* Here I Stand. *The full text of his statement follows.*)

The other day while I was out for a walk near my home here in New York, one of our folks—as it often happens—came over to pump my hand and said: "Paul, it's good to see you! Man, where have you been, and what are you doing, and how are you feeling, and what have you got to say?" We walked along together, chatting like old friends who hadn't seen each other for a long time. While I was trying to answer all the man's questions, I recalled with an inward smile that the editors of many leading magazines have had their own long list of questions for reporters to ask me. However, since my return home from Europe some eight months ago I have declined to give any interviews or to make any public statements.

The fact is, I have been resting and recovering my health and strength after a rather prolonged illness. But while I am not yet able to resume public life and activities, I think it is time that I said a few words through the Negro press to the many persons who, like the friendly strangers on the street, have been wondering what has happened to me.

First, let me warmly thank all those who have expressed good wishes for my recovery; your kind concern has been the best of all medicines. I am happy to say that I have regained the weight I had lost in my period of exhaustion, and I'm feeling better. My doctors assure me that I am on the road to recovery.

While I must continue my temporary retirement from public life, I am, of course, deeply involved with the great upsurge of our people. Like all of you, my heart has been filled with admiration for the many thousands of Negro freedom fighters and their white associates who are waging the battle for civil rights throughout the country and especially in the South. Along with the pride has been the great sorrow and righteous wrath we all shared when the evil forces of white supremacy brutally murdered the Birmingham children and some of our finest heroes, like Medgar Evers and the three young men of Mississippi.

For me there has also been the sorrow that I have felt on returning home and experiencing the loss of persons who for many long years were near and dear to me—my beloved older brother, the Reverend Benjamin C. Robeson, who passed away while I was gone; and my longtime colleague and coworker, Dr. W.E.B. Du Bois, foremost statesman and scholar of our people, who died last year in Ghana. And now has come deep grief at the death of Ben Davis, a precious friend whose indomitable courage and dedication to the fight for freedom has always been a glowing inspiration for me.

"Many thousand gone . . ." but we, the living, are more firmly resolved: "No more driver's lash for me!" The dedicated lives of all who have fallen in our long uphill march shall be fulfilled, for truly "We *shall* overcome." The issue of *freedom now* for Negro Americans has become the main issue confronting this nation, and the peoples of the whole world are looking to see it finally resolved.

When I wrote in my book, *Here I Stand*, in 1958 that "the time is now," some people thought that perhaps my watch was fast (and maybe it was a little), but most of us seem to be running on the same time— now. The "power of Negro action," of which I then wrote, has changed from an idea to a reality that is manifesting itself throughout our land. The concept of mass militancy, of mass action, is no longer deemed "too radical" in Negro life. The idea that black Americans should see that the fight for a "Free World" begins at home—a shocking idea when expressed in Paris in 1949—no longer is challenged in our communities. The "hot summer" of struggle for equal rights has replaced the "cold war" abroad as the concern of our people.

It is especially heartening to me to see the active and often heroic part that leading Negro artists—singers, actors, writers, comedians, musicians—are playing today in the freedom struggle. Today it is the Negro artist who does *not* speak out who is considered to be out of line, and even the white audiences have largely come around to accepting the fact that the Negro artist is—and has every right to be—quite "controversial."

Yes, it is good to see all these transformations. It is heartening also to see that despite differences in program and personalities among Negro leadership, the concept of a united front of all forces and viewpoints is gaining ground.

There is more—much more—that needs to be done, of course, before we can reach our goals. But if we cannot as yet sing, "Thank God Almighty, we're free at last," we surely can all sing together: "Thank God Almighty, we're *moving!*"

PAUL ROBESON

New York,
August 28, 1964